Acting Essentials

Acting Essentials

or

Just Say Your Lines Like You Mean Them and Don't Bump into the Scenery

A Practical, Beginning Acting Handbook

ALEX GOLSON

Orange Coast College

Boston   Burr Ridge, IL   Dubuque, IA   Madison, WI   New York
San Francisco   St. Louis   Bangkok   Bogotá   Caracas   Kuala Lumpur
Lisbon   London   Madrid   Mexico City   Milan   Montreal   New Delhi
Santiago   Seoul   Singapore   Sydney   Taipei   Toronto

McGraw-Hill Higher Education

A Division of The **McGraw-Hill** Companies

6 7 8 9 0 BAH/BAH 0 9 8 7 6 5 4 3

Library of Congress Cataloging-in-Publication Data
Golson, Alex.
    Acting essentials, or, Just say your lines like you mean them and don't bump into the scenery: a practical beginning acting handbook / Alex Golson
        p.   cm.
    Includes bibliographical references (p.   ) and index.

    ISBN-13: 978-0-7674-2251-2
    ISBN-10: 0-7674-2251-1

    1. Acting.   I. Title.   II. Title: Acting essentials.   III. Title: Just say your lines like you
mean them and don't bump into the scenery.
    PN2061.G645 2002
    792'.028—dc21   2001030042

Sponsoring editor, Janet M. Beatty: *production editor,* Carla White Kirschenbaum; *manuscript editor,* Patricia Ohlenroth; *text designer,* Anne Flanagan; *design manager and cover designer,* Jean Mailander; *art editor,* Robin Mouat; *illustrator,* Larry Daste; *manufacturing manager,* Randy Hurst. Cover image by Larry Daste. The text was set in 12/16 Tekton by Emma Ghiselli and printed on 50# Butte des Morts by Banta Book Group.

www.mhhe.com

To the four teachers who taught me how to teach

Ashley Carr
Robert Cohen
John Ferzacca
William Purkiss

Did ya ever notice how much acting
teachers like to name drop?

Preface

Learning how to act should be physically, mentally, and emotionally challenging and, above all, fun. It is challenging because you are exploring and experiencing your body, mind, and emotions in very new, often difficult, and personally expanding ways. It is fun because there is simply nothing more liberating and empowering than using your imagination and creative powers to pretend and to play.

Too often in actor training, as in most educational pursuits, we teachers forget the value fun, creative enjoyment, and true joy can have in the act of learning complex—and sometimes formidable—new skills. For a student to really embrace and to fully commit to the demands of learning to act, that student has to enjoy doing it. Discipline and a good solid work ethic are, of course, extremely important for any student. But what has become clear to me after twenty-five years of teaching beginning actors is that no one can force any student actors to sustain any long-term interest or discipline if they are confused, uninspired, or simply not finding the very personal reward of having fun.

Without a doubt the most certain way to make sure students are *not* enjoying learning to act is to load them down with too many theories, techniques, and methodologies. I wrote this book specifically to promote the idea that in early actor training everything should be kept to the absolute essentials. Students will be introduced to the essentials of the craft of acting in this book and explore them through an enriching series of exercises and pithy pieces of advice.

Instructors, I hope, will appreciate the flexibility the book affords, with more than 100 exercises clearly identified according to the skills they focus on as well as a host of solid script analysis tools. It also doesn't hurt one bit that we've kept the book as light and as affordable as we could.

Acknowledgments

This book owes much to many people. First and foremost I wish to thank my graduate acting and directing teacher, Robert Cohen, for his great help and advice on many occasions. Ashley Carr was my master teacher in graduate school. He literally taught me how to be a teacher. He also showed me, by example, how teaching can be a great art. My two community college instructors when I was a student at Orange Coast College were William Purkiss and John Ferzacca. They have truly been my mentors for more than thirty years. They both are remarkable and inspirational men of the theatre. Two other inspirational teachers kept whispering in my ear as I wrote: Barbara Van Holt and Bruce Dern. The words, thoughts, and advice of these six people are found often in this book.

There are maybe a half dozen original ideas in this handbook; the rest of the ideas are variations of what I have learned from some very remarkable acting teachers. They are, in chronological order: Arlee Higbee, Barbara Van Holt, Sheila Goldes, Robert Wentz, Lucian Scott, Jack Holland, Bill Purkiss, John Ferzacca, Lee Strasberg, Bruce Dern, Gerald S. O'Laughlin, Peggy Feury, William Traylor, Michael O'Sullivan, William Ball, Francis Lee McCain, Howard Berman, Edwin Duerr, Alvin Keller, Kirk Mee, Dean Hess, Donald Henry, Robert Rence, Ron Deib, Mike Macpherson, Joseph Arnold, Ashley Carr, Robert Cohen, Stuart Duckworth, Brewster Mason, Clayton Garrison, William Needles, Patrick Stewart, Ben Kingsley, Richard Pasco, Cecily Berry, Doug Rowe, Eric Morris, Warren Robertson, Donna Soto-Morettini, Jon Sidoli, Sharon Harwood, David Scaglione, Joan McGillis, Phyllis Gitlin, and Rick Golson. Thank you. I am blessed to have known you all.

I cannot imagine a more professional or better publishing team than all the people at Mayfield Publishing Company. They include: Jan Beatty, Senior Editor; Carla Kirschenbaum, Senior Production Editor; Patricia Ohlenroth, copyeditor; Larry Daste, illustrator; Jean Mailander, Senior Designer; Robin Mouat, Art Editor; Emma Ghiselli, Associate Art Editor; and Randy Hurst, Manufacturing Manager.

The comments and suggestions I received from the reviewers added greatly to the organization, content, and shaping of this book. They include: Robert Dunkerley, Community College of Southern Nevada; Phyllis B. Gitlin, Riverside Community College; Dale McFadden, Indiana University; C. Tim Quinn, Fresno City College; and Andrew Ryder, Seattle Pacific University.

Thank you all so much.

Contents

1

Getting Ready to Act: or I'm Not Going to Have to Pretend I'm a Tree, Am I? And What Is It I'm Supposed to Do with My Hands? I Said, What Am I Supposed to Do with My Hands?   1

2

Things You Should Know about Acting So It Doesn't Look Like You Don't Know What You Are Doing   25

3

Getting Yourself Going and Your Creative Juices Flowing   48

4

Exploring the Script and Scene   60

5

Character, Emotion, and the Rehearsal Process 84

6

Now Add the Audience 101

7

Tips, More Advice, Secrets, Things That Work, Strange Things Actors Do, and a Few Final Words 105

List of Exercises

Chapter 4: Exploring the Script and Scene   60

Introduction

Acting is easy, but sometimes it's real hard for me to do easy things.

—Hal Golson, age 5, on acting in his first play, *Stuart Little*.

You Have Always Been an Actor

Learning to act is not like learning a new skill, such as how to do yoga, play the violin, or operate a computer. You have been developing the skills you need to act since you were a baby. Every time you tried to communicate, every time you played make-believe, every time you played dress up, every time you told a lie, every time you covered up an emotion, every time you manipulated your parents or teacher to get what you wanted, you were acting. We use acting skills all the time. This small handbook will show you how to recognize and further develop those skills.

Less Is More

This handbook is an attempt to present only the very basic acting theory, advice, and exercises that a student needs to know to begin acting or to prepare a character. I have only presented the basics because it is my true belief that too much acting theory and advice can, sometimes, be counterproductive and confusing for the beginning actor.

Keep It Simple

Acting is not a mysterious process. As I have already stated, you have been acting all of your life.

If you read this handbook, take note of its observations, and follow its simple and straightforward exercises and advice, you will see yourself grow and develop a logical methodology that will help you become mentally and physically ready to act, analyze a scene, and prepare a character. Eventually, acting will seem as simple and natural as just saying your lines like you mean them and not bumping into the scenery.

Where Did the Subtitle Come From?

Variations of the aphorism "Just say your lines like you mean them and don't bump into the scenery" have been attributed to several actors, including Spencer Tracy, Frank Sinatra, Humphrey Bogart, Helen Hayes, Bette Davis, James Cagney, and Noel Coward. Who said it does not really matter. The real meaning of it does.

Acting should be kept as simple and rational as possible. Just do it and believe in all you are doing. At the same time, be aware and in control of what you are doing and how you are doing it. In other words, just say your lines like you mean them and don't bump into the scenery.

1

Getting Ready to Act

Or

I'm Not Going to Have to Pretend I'm a Tree, Am I?
And What Is It I'm Supposed to Do with My Hands?
I Said, What Am I Supposed to Do with My Hands?

SENSORY, PHYSICAL, AND VOCAL AWARENESS

This first chapter explores and introduces you to yourself. It is short on advice and theory and long on exercises that will open you up and help you become aware of your imagination, memory, and physical and vocal capability and potential.

There is no order or step-by-step process through which you must work in this first section. That is to say: You don't first work on sensory awareness, then move to physical awareness, and then finally work on vocalization. All of these areas should be worked on at the same time. Physical awareness will support vocal and sensory awareness and vice versa.

You will get the best results from the exercises in this book by repeating them many times. Each time you do, you will discover interesting and useful things about your senses, body, and voice; and you will begin to open yourself up to an acute new personal awareness. Developing a sharp sense of awareness is the first and most essential step in becoming an actor.

WAKING UP YOUR IMAGINATION, MEMORY, AND FIVE SENSES

Rarely do you really get to eat or drink what you appear to be eating or drinking onstage or on camera. Apple juice or iced tea becomes whiskey; water is vodka or gin; mashed up banana appears as a number of foods. You also are rarely in the actual environment described in the script. Almost never is the set the same temperature or undergoing the same weather conditions as suggested in the script. The list of sensory challenges for the actor goes on and on. It is your job to remember and re-create what you are supposed to be smelling, touching, feeling, lifting, seeing, tasting, and hearing. It must appear that you are really doing these things and that you are actually reacting to a received stimulus.

Such reactions are best achieved by using sense memory. Sense memory works through the memory and imagination to re-create how an actual physical experience feels.

When I was nineteen, I auditioned for and was accepted in the very first class at the Lee Strasberg Theatre Institute. There, I had several remarkable teachers including Lee Strasberg, Peggy Feury, and Bruce Dern. It was an excellent learning experience. Growing up, my heroes were all the famous method actors like Marlon Brando, Paul Newman, and James Dean, who all studied with Lee Strasberg. Arriving at the institute, I could hardly wait to really get into it! I wanted to plunge deeply into my soul and drag out all of the deep, dark, and powerful emotions I just knew were hidden somewhere inside me. However, my amazing, potentially deep and sensitive emotional life had to wait awhile.

All I remember doing for the first six weeks was trying to imagine holding a coffee cup in my hand—I'm sure we did other things, but that is all I can remember. It got so that I knew all there was about that cup. I spent much more quality time with that stupid cup than I did with my girlfriend. I even started dreaming about it. To this day, I can imagine and sensorially re-create that cup at any time of day or night under any circumstances at a moment's notice. All that said, it is now your turn to imagine holding a cup and to activate your sense memory with a few exercises.

 ## The Cup Exercise

Hold out your hand. Imagine you are holding a cup. Imagine its shape, size, and weight. Move the fingers of your other hand around it. Notice any imperfections or bumps. Spend several minutes experiencing this cup. Now imagine putting something into it, like coffee or orange juice. Feel the added weight. Smell it, taste it. Feel the heat or cold. Now, spend hours and hours and hours and hours doing this and you will be just like all of the other people who went through the Strasberg Institute or The Actors Studio, where Lee Strasberg taught his method-acting classes.

 ## The Lemon Exercise

Imagine you are cutting up a lemon. Feel it, smell it, and touch it. Can you feel your mouth start to pucker as you imagine cutting that lemon? Imagine eating, drinking, or preparing other foods and beverages with strong tastes, such as:

- Chocolate
- Strong cheese
- Salt water
- A sugar cube
- Coffee
- Milk
- Hot sauce
- Whiskey
- A pickle
- Lemonade
- Tea

 ## Old Room Sense Memory

Sit and get comfortable. Close your eyes. Breathe and relax. Try to remember a room from your past, someplace that has special memories and where you spent a lot of time. Scan the room quickly. Try to get an overall sense of it. Now go through the room with your memory and re-create what you smelled, what you tasted, what you felt (touched), what you heard, and what you saw (shapes, sizes, colors, and distances). Be as specific as you can. Note if anything you remember conjures up any forgotten emotions or memories.

 ## Standing in the Weather Exercise

Stand with your feet at least as wide as your shoulders. Close your eyes. With your sense memory re-create specific times when you stood outside:

- In a light rain
- During a light breeze
- During a heat wave
- During a blizzard
- In a heavy rain
- During a heavy wind
- During a light snow

Be as specific as possible. Use all five of your senses to re-create these experiences.

 ## Object Passing Exercise

Either in a circle in class or one-on-one with a partner, pass several imagined objects around or back and forth. Some suggestions for objects include a ten-pound sack of potatoes, a pillow, an air-filled balloon, a basketball, a heavy book, a hot cup of coffee, an ice cube, a thirty-pound bag of ice, a piece of delicate crystal, or a huge boulder. Work with your partner(s). Really try to simulate the experience as closely as possible. Use all of your senses and your whole body.

 ## Imagined Tug-of-War Exercise

You and your partner face each other. Stand two to five feet apart. Pretend you are both holding a 15–20-foot-long rope. Have a

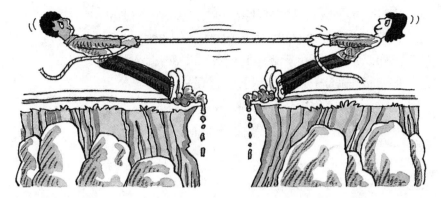

tug-of-war game. Use your entire body including your voice. This exercise should last at least three minutes. Work with your partner. Remember, the rope doesn't stretch. No one wins or loses in this game. It must end in a tie.

Raise the Stakes

Do the imagined tug-of-war exercise again, but this time raise the stakes of the game. When you raise the stakes, you'll feel your body work harder if your imagination is strong enough. So, as you play the game again, imagine the following obstacles between you and your partner:

- A mud puddle
- A 500-foot drop-off
- Poisonous snakes
- A fire pit

Shake out at the end of each tug-of-war. Keep breathing and feel the energy in your body when you finish each game.

LET'S GET PHYSICAL

Acting is a very physical activity. Ultimately, everything you do, including thinking, speaking, moving, and using your five senses, involves your body. To that end, you must:

Become very aware of how your body works and feels.

Understand your physical strengths and limitations.

Explore how your mind and body interact.

Learn how you can relax and control tension.

Discover how you can energize yourself.

Gain great endurance and stamina.

The following exercises will explore all these physical elements and help you get ready to act.

Body Scan Exercise

Most of the time, we live our lives in a state of limited consciousness. We rarely take time to "just be" and to truly experience "being." For the next five to ten minutes, try to let go of everything you need and have to do and just experience yourself.

To begin this exercise, stand with your feet at least as wide apart as your shoulders. Make yourself as comfortable as you can. Loosen your clothes and belt—anything interfering with your comfort. Close your eyes. First, simply scan your entire body. Feel it being and working. Feel:

- Your heart beating
- Your blood flowing
- Your muscles holding you up
- Your clothes against your skin
- Your breath

Take a long time to feel yourself breathe. Now, scan your body for any spots of tension. Are you holding tensions in your neck muscles, in your jaw, forehead, arms, or anywhere else? Go through your five senses. What do you feel? What do you smell? What do you taste? Move your tongue around your mouth. Is there a taste to the air? What do you hear? Now, open your eyes. What do you see? Look around you. Try to notice something new, something you had not really noticed before. Scan the whole room using all of your senses.

It is important for everyone, especially the creative person, to go off automatic pilot once and a while and to really take time to experience one's body and the world around us. This sensitivity is the foundation of physical awareness.

Just Standing There Exercise

Go up on stage or in front of the class. Just stand there and look around you. Look at the audience. Stay up there at least 5 minutes. When you are done, ask yourself these questions:

- How long did it feel like I was up there?
- Did I feel awkward?
- Did I know what to do with my hands or how to stand? Did I feel like adjusting my clothes?
- How comfortable did I feel just standing there?

Just Do Something Exercise

Stand before the group again. This time, have a very specific task to accomplish. Try these tasks:

- Look at the audience. Count the different hair colors. Make a mental list of the most common colors and the least common.

- Take a pad of paper and divide 837 by 323.

- Try to remember, then make a list of all the elementary, intermediate, and high school teachers you have had. Make another list of your favorites.

Let's see, second grade was Mrs. Hendrick, third grade was Mr. Spenser. . .

- Take inventory of everything you see in the room, such as the number of lights, seats, people, and floorboards.

Now, mentally or in a discussion with the group, explore how you felt the first time and the second time on stage. For most people, the time goes by much faster and they become much less self-conscious when they must concentrate on doing a difficult or consuming task.

Acting is about staying focused, staying aware, and physically attempting to accomplish one task at a time. In this state, you should be well aware of what you need to do physically to complete your assigned task, but at the same time, you must not overtly be watching yourself or self-conscious about doing your task. Just do it! Don't worry about how you do it! If you know what you need to accomplish, your body will tend to take care of itself. It's much like in baseball when your main job is to keep your eye on the ball. If you watch the ball, your body will usually do what is necessary to try to hit or catch it.

The Figure Eight Exercise

This exercise is incredibly simple, yet it works better than any other exercise I have ever tried on exploring just how your body moves.

Hold your right or left hand comfortably in front of you. Working from your wrists, let your hand do small, slow, and fluid figure eights. Do this for one or two minutes. Now, use your other hand. Use both hands at the same time. Have them go in the same direction, then opposite directions. Next, do figure eights with your arms. Now, use your feet and legs as you make figure eights. Keep breathing while you do this exercise. If you hold your breath too long, you may get a little dizzy. If you get dizzy, stop the exercise and sit or lie down. Now, start using other parts of your body:

- Your shoulders
- Your fingers
- Your head
- Your tongue

- The top part of your body • The bottom half

Go through your whole body. Isolate areas again. This should take a good five minutes. Shake out when you are done.

Your Personal Center

For a variety of reasons, including weight, height, the length of one's legs in relationship to one's torso, and physical coordination, everyone walks and moves differently. One other factor that can have a great influence on how you move, is called your personal center. Your personal center is that area in your body from which all of your movement seems to originate. It can also be called your center of gravity or your center of balance.

Your personal center could be near your belt area, up high in your chest, in your groin area, or even in your legs. A person with a personal center in the center of their body will tend to be very balanced and physically grounded. A person with a personal center high in the chest area might appear to be clumsy or gangly. A person with a personal center in the groin area may appear animalistic, macho, threatening, or seductive.

Once you become aware of your center, you can actually move it. You personally may have a middle center. Try putting it up in your chest. See how you move. Now, put your center in your groin or legs. How does that change your movement? By changing how you move, you can change how you feel about yourself and your body. This, of course, is a useful tool to understand how a character that is different from yourself moves and views him- or herself.

 Personal Center Exercise

Get up in front of the class. Try to walk and do a physical activity like picking up items on the floor. Have the class discuss where they think your personal center is.

During the next class or after a break, get up in front of the class again. Do the same activity as before, but this time consciously change your center. Have the class discuss any changes they see in your walk and movements.

 ## Personal Center Observation Exercise

Go somewhere where there are many people walking and doing a variety of activities. Try to identify each person's personal center and how that effects how they move. Also speculate why particular people have their center where it is. It could be related to their body image, age, occupation, type of shoes, health, or the fact that people are watching them.

 ## Big Space, Little Space

This exercise will help you stretch, warm up, and become aware of the space that your body occupies.

1. Shake out and stretch your body slowly.
2. Shake out again.
3. Bounce up and down a little and slowly stretch out again.
4. Slowly try to make your body as tall as you can.
5. Come back to normal size.
6. Slowly try to make your body as wide as possible.
7. Come back to normal size.
8. Slowly try to make your body take up as much space as possible, making it both tall and wide at the same time.
9. Gradually shrink down to normal size.
10. Now, slowly shrink even further—get smaller and smaller and smaller. Try to take up as little space as possible.
11. Now, start growing again, and this time do not stop when you reach your normal size. Start stretching to take up as much space as possible.

Slowly repeat the exercise three or four times, but with each repetition decrease the time it takes to contract and expand. Always keep breathing while you work. Shake out when you are done.

Ball of Energy Exercise

This exercise works on developing physical awareness and using your imagination and your physical energy.

Stand with your feet at least as wide apart as your shoulders. You may wish to close your eyes, but it isn't necessary. With your imagination, feel a ball of energy (electricity or light, if you wish) about the size of your fist in your right foot. The ball of energy makes your foot tingle and vibrate slightly. The ball begins to move up, toward your ankle, your shin, and your calf and knee. It continues up on your right side to the top of your head. As it moves up your right side, it makes each area over which it passes vibrate. After it reaches the top of your head, it begins moving down to your left side until it reaches your left foot. Your whole body should be vibrating slightly. Now, double the intensity of the vibration. Double it again. Get your whole body shaking.

Stop!

Now isolate areas. Just your legs. Just your hands. The top half of your body. The bottom half. The front half. Back half. Your whole body. Keep breathing throughout and slowly stretch out when you are finished.

A Good, Full Body Stretch

Stand with feet shoulders' width apart. Keep your heels on the ground and keep breathing throughout the exersize. Shake out.

1. Reach with your hands and arms straight up and try to reach the ceiling.

2. Relax your arms. Let them drop.

3. Reach up again.

4. This time, release just your hands.

5. Try to touch the ceiling with your wrists.

6. Release your forearms. Try to touch the ceiling with your elbows.

7. Release your arms. Try to touch the ceiling with your head.

8. Release your head. Let it plop down on your chest.

9. Try to touch the ceiling with your shoulders.

10. Release your shoulders.

11. Roll your head around your neck and shoulders. Be careful not to push down. Lift your head up slightly as it rolls past your spine. You don't want to compress the muscles in the back of your neck or your spine.

12. Let your head plop down on your chest again. Imagine your head weighs fifty pounds. Let it pull the top half of your body down. As you begin to bend down, put your arms out in front of you.

13. Form a circle with your arms, letting your fingertips just touch. This will create a curve in your torso and stretch your spine. Don't lock your knees. Keep them slightly bent.

14. Straighten up.

15. Move up and down several times. Be sure you keep your fingertips touching.

16. Come up one last time. Feel your head float up and slightly forward.

17. Now stretch up once again with your arms. Keep your heels on the ground. Pretend you are picking oranges or apples or that you are a cat stretching. First stretch with your right arm, then your left. Rock back and forth, right, then left, stretching one or two inches taller with each reach.

Shrinking Room Exercise

You and your partner are in a small room: 7 X 7 X 7. It slowly begins to shrink. Both of you are forced to push back the walls, but at first you can't. The room compresses all the way down to 2½ X 2½ X 2½. Finally, you start pushing the walls back. You win and you are safe.

This exercise explores goals, imagination, and working with your partner. It is an excellent physical warm-up.

 ## Music Video Exercise #1

Choose your favorite song. Play it without actually singing or lip synching. Act out the story.

 ## Music Video Exercise #2

Choose another favorite popular song. This time, wear earphones. Only you can hear the music. In silence, act out the story. Try not to exaggerate and keep everything as realistic as possible.

This is not a guessing game, but see if the class knows the song. If not, play the song and ask for comments.

 ## Children's Story Exercise

Read a short children's story to the class but do not read it aloud. Instead, read silently and convey the story with movements, props, and gestures.

Learning to Relax and Recognizing Physical Tension

Tension can be a major impediment to your ability to use your body effectively. You must find ways to consciously recognize and eliminate (or at least minimize) tension in your body.

The Best Relaxation Exercise Ever

Yawn.

Make yourself yawn. At first, fake it to get yourself going. After a couple of tries you will really be yawning. This will immediately begin to relax you. Try this yawning exercise just before you start performing. It's the best and quickest relaxation exercise there is.

 ## The Other Best Relaxation Exercise Ever

Smile!

Even if you are tired and having a lousy day, fake a great big smile. Trick yourself into feeling better. With this trick, you can't help but relax a little.

 ## Cheer Exercise

If a smile helps you relax, why not take it a step further and start cheering. Jump up and down; yell: Hooray! Yippee! Yabba dabba doo! Everything is great! We won! I am the champion, my friend! Do this for a good solid minute and you *will* relax and feel better.

 ## Tense and Relax Exercise

Sit in a comfortable chair or lie down on the floor. Get as comfortable as possible. Scan your body for tension. If you find any knots or areas of tension, mentally will those knots or areas to release and relax.

Put your concentration on your feet. Slowly tense the muscles in your feet. Slowly release the tension and relax the muscles.

Move up your body. Tense and relax your:

1. Ankles, shins, and calves
2. Knees and thighs

3. Pelvis and butt

4. Stomach and lower back

5. Chest and upper back

6. Shoulders

7. Arms and hands

8. Neck

9. Face and skull

Rescan your body for any tension. If you find an area of tension, re-tense and relax. Then, just sit or lie there for a few minutes. Breathe and don't move.

Imagined Journey Exercise

Do the tense and relax exercise. When you have completed the exercise, sit for a moment with your eyes closed. Now, using your imagination feel yourself float up and away. This makes you feel very free, relaxed, and safe. Imagine you are floating a few feet off the ground. Now, imagine you are in a very long hallway. You are floating along the hallway. It feels fun, relaxing, and safe. After a minute or so, you come to the end of the hallway. You float out. You don't know where you are at first but you feel very safe and relaxed. Soon you realize you are at your favorite place in the world, maybe a forest, a park, a beach, or your room. Using your senses, experience this place. What do you hear? What do you smell, taste, touch, and see? You should feel very relaxed and at peace. At your own speed, let your mind return to the present.

Shower Exercise

Stand with your feet at least shoulders' width apart. Close your eyes. Pretend you are taking a shower. Hear the water, feel the temperature, taste the water, smell the soap and water. Now, see the water hit you. As the water hits you, allow it to release the tension in each area.

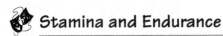 **Stamina and Endurance**

Playing a leading role in a play or film takes great physical stamina. A stage role like Richard III, St. Joan, or Harold Hill (The Music Man) can take as much energy as running a 10K or even a half-marathon race. Actors must be in as good a shape as possible.

When I was an actor in New York, without question the one main topic among all the actors whenever we got together to socialize was the latest gym, aerobics, or yoga class. Professional actors must always be vigilant about keeping their bodies in the best physical shape possible. Being in good shape can often determine whether or not you will be cast in a role, and thus whether you can pay your rent.

There are no one or two exercises that will get you in shape. Being at your highest physical potential is a conscious lifestyle choice. Some of the things you need to do to be in top physical condition include eating regular meals of good, nutritious foods and regularly exercising. Include aerobic types of exercise in your routine to get your heart going, such as jogging, bicycling, swimming, and playing racquetball. Also do strength-building and flexibility exercises, such as yoga, tai chi, dance, and weight training routines. You must also get enough sleep and maintain regular sleep habits. Finally, don't engage in such physically and mentally self-destructive behavior as using illegal drugs, drinking alcohol, or smoking. Treat your body with respect. Treat it as if your life and your paycheck depended on it.

LET'S GET VOCAL

Projection, Enunciation, and Articulation

Projection: To say words and lines loud enough to be heard

Enunciation: To pronounce words clearly and distinctly

Articulation: To speak sounds clearly, especially consonants

When you project your voice, enunciate your words and articulate
your consonants, you have one goal in mind: to be heard and understood. You say words loudly, clearly, and with emphasis because
what you have to say is important. You speak up and speak clearly
because if you don't, you won't get what you want. You speak so
the whole world around you can hear you. You do this because the
people to whom you speak are those who can get you what you
want and need. In other words, you make sure
they can hear you and understand you
because it is important for you to
be heard and understood. If for
some reason you cannot
be heard or under-
stood, first work
on making what
you say and how
you say it more
compelling. The
best example I
can think of is
this: If you are

*And a cheeseburger, please. I repeat cheeseburger.
Cheese for cheese, burger for burger.*

going through a fast-food drive-thru and you really want a cheeseburger, you make sure the person on the other end hears and understands the word *cheeseburger.* Make all of your lines as
important as your order of that cheeseburger. If you really want
something enough, you will be heard and understood.

Supporting Your Voice

You produce sound by pushing outgoing air across your vocal
cords, which causes them to vibrate. These vibrations create
sound.

Your vocal cords work very hard and are really pretty sturdy, but they can be overworked and strained by putting too much stress on them. If you were to use your vocal cords without supporting them and minimizing stress, the chances are pretty good that after an hour or two of talking you would get a sore throat or begin to lose your voice.

Believe it or not, to support your vocal cords you must learn how to use your stomach muscles. I have really never seen my diaphragm (or anyone else's for that matter). I take it as a matter of faith and reason that I have one. The diaphragm is a large internal muscle attached to the lower ribs. It separates the chest from the abdomen. When you take a full breath, your diaphragm moves downward. When you breathe out your diaphragm relaxes. Most of this happens automatically, and you do not have much control over it. However, you can take a good full breath by consciously using your stomach muscle to breathe, which supports your diaphragm. This is the most natural and efficient way of breathing. This will maximize your air intake and will give you good air flow through your vocal cords. It will also help your cords feel supported and able to work efficiently and with a minimum of stress.

Here are a few exercises to help you understand how to give your vocal cords good breath support through the use of your diaphragm and stomach muscles. Do these exercises daily for two or three weeks.

Stomach Muscle Breathing Exercise

1. Stand with your feet as wide as your shoulders.
2. Put your hand on the top half of your stomach.
3. Without breathing consciously, stick your stomach out then squeeze it in. Watch and feel your hand and stomach move back and forth.
4. Now take a deep breath. As you breathe in, consciously stick out your stomach. As you breathe out tense and contract

your stomach muscles. Do this several times. You will be taking in a lot of air, which you may not be used to. If you start feeling dizzy, sit down for a minute or two.

5. Now, put your other hand on your collarbone and chest.

6. Take several deep breaths. As you breathe in and out your chest may expand a bit, but make sure it does not move up and down. Your stomach should be expanding and relaxed as the air comes in and tensed as the air goes out.

7. Now, take another deep breath and as the air goes out tense your stomach muscles and try to produce a sound through your vocal cords, such as "aww." This sound should be half air and half sound. Do this several times.

8. Now, make the sound using a lot of support from your stomach and diaphragm, but do not sound "breathy."

Pant Exercise

Put your hand on your stomach and pant like a dog. See your hand and stomach bounce back and forth.

Quarterback Exercise

Pretend you are a football quarterback starting a play. Say "hut, hut, hut." Bounce them out. Each time feel your stomach tense up. Use a lot of breath and each time increase the volume of breath you expel and speed at which you release it.

Yawn and Sigh

With your hand on your stomach fake a yawn. See your hand and stomach move outward. Now sigh. Feel your stomach tense and see your stomach and hand move inward.

Here are a few more exercises that can help you speak with precision and help you warm up your body.

The Lips, the Teeth, and the Tip of the Tongue Exercise

This exercise helps you wake up your mouth so you can speak clearly and with precision.

1. Stick out your tongue. Bring it back in. Now move it back and forth five to six times. Move your tongue around your mouth and teeth for at least one full minute.

2. Stretch your mouth way out. Now pucker it up. Do this back and forth for one full minute saying "oohh" and "aahh" as you do.

3. Chew as if you have ten pieces of gum in your mouth. Let your jaw drop open. Using the palm of your hand, massage your jaw muscles. Keeping your jaw open, open and close your lips.

4. Blow out making motorboat sounds with your lips.

5. Let your mouth drop open more. Shake your jaw and mouth while saying "aahh."

6. Now, quickly go through the sequence again: Move your tongue. Stretch and pucker. Chew. Drop your jaw. Massage your jaw. Make the motorboat noise. Shake your jaw.

Consonant Alphabet Exercise

Go through each consonant sound. Really exaggerate and explode each sound.

Baa	Baa	Baa
Caa	Caa	Caa

Daa	Daa	Daa
Faa	Faa	Faa
Gaa	Gaa	Gaa
Jaa	Jaa	Jaa
Laa	Laa	Laa
Maa	Maa	Maa
Naa	Naa	Naa
Paa	Paa	Paa
Qua	Qua	Qua
Raa	Raa	Raa
Saa	Saa	Saa
Taa	Taa	Taa
Vaa	Vaa	Vaa
Zaa	Zaa	Zaa

Long List Exercise

Write out a list of seven to fifteen items. Memorize the list. Decide on an immediate goal. Then relate the list to your partner. Work on a vocal crescendo by saying the name of each item as if it were more important than the one before. You may start out relating the list with a line like:

- I want...
- Why don't you go get me...
- My favorite things are...

A Good Simple Seven-Minute Physical and Vocal Warm-Up

1. Stand with your feet at least as wide as your shoulders. Take three slow deep breaths. Shake out your body, slowly. Take three more breaths. Shake out again.

2. Imagine in your right foot there is a ball of energy about the size of your fist. It makes your foot shake like it is being slightly electrified. With your imagination, feel the ball of energy move up to your head. Now, imagine it is moving down the left side. It is energizing your whole body. Increase the level several times until you are shaking your whole body.

Stop.

3. Now, isolate areas such as your feet, your arms, the top half of your body, the bottom half, the right side, and the left side. Do this for two to three minutes. Breathe several times. Stretch your body. Keep your heels on the ground and reach upward as high as you can, stretching like a cat, first with your right hand, then with your left. Breathe.

4. Now, imagine someone or something in front of you. Have a fight with that person or thing. Hit it. Kick it. Scratch it. Yell at it. Then, shake out and breathe.

5. Now, pretend you have ten to fifteen pieces of gum in your mouth. Chew. Open your mouth and move your tongue around. Stretch your face out. Pucker up your face. Go back and forth from stretch to pucker. Now, chew again. Let your jaw drop open. Message your jaw with the palm of your hand.

6. Now, close your lips, and blow out, keeping your jaw loose.

    Now, with a loose jaw, say, "Bah." Say it a couple dozen times.

    Now, say each of the following several times: "Bah Dah," "Gah," "Tah," and "Gah Tah." Now, put it all together and repeat "Bah, dah, gah, tah" many times. Change the consonants and say:

    - "Fah, Dah, Gah, Tah"
    - "Lah, Dah, Gah, Tah"
    - "Rah, Dah Gah, Tah"
    - "Nah, Dah Gah, Tah"

Breathe and shake out.

7. Supporting your voice with your diaphragm, say with the lowest tone you can use: "Ooooohhhhh," using a lot of breath. In the middle of your range say "Aaaaaahhhhh," using a lot of breath. At the top of your natural range, say "Hey." Now, in your falsetto or head voice, or in a tiny squeak say "Weeeee." Now, go up and down your range several times using "Oooh, Aahh, Hey, Weee." Breathe and shake out. Stand quietly and feel your breath.

8. Now, imagine being in a shower. Feel the water on your body. Where the water hits you, you are relaxed. Feel the tension flow away.

   Now, stretch and take three big breaths. Shake out.

   After this exercise, you should be pretty well warmed up and ready to perform or rehearse.

Twenty-two Tongue Twisters to Try

Tongue twisters take time to master. Some make your mouth magically malleable. Try these tongue twisters.

1. Specific Pacific
2. Nuke New York
3. You need to nuke unique New York
4. Apple Annie Apple Ann
5. Betty Boop beat Bob
6. New York is near Newark, Newark is near New York
7. Some simpletons sun Sunday somedays
8. Dumb Danes definitely don't do division
9. Try to triple Tom's two step
10. Bigger bakers bake better buttery bread
11. Some sellers see several cellar doors
12. Seattle sometimes seems sunny

13. Toy boat don't float
14. Nightly news now 9:19
15. 'Cause Chris can carry kangaroos
16. Little Larry likes lollipops
17. Molly might marry Monday morning
18. Quickly, quietly, carefully
19. Let Laura languish lightly
20. Giraffes gulp green grass
21. Yip hip dip zip
22. Sir Nicholas Gawsey hath for succor sent and so hath Clifton. I'll to Clifton straight. (Henry IV, part 1, act 5, scene 4)

2

Things You Should Know about Acting So It Doesn't Look Like You Don't Know What You Are Doing

In this chapter, you will explore the essential information, advice, and exercises that will enable you to focus, behave, and think like an actor. The following is a list of ethics, points of etiquette, and traditions that you should incorporate into your work as an actor.

ACTOR ETHICS, ETIQUETTE, AND TRADITIONS

Don't relate to others like a prima donna or a star.

Treat all other actors, designers, and production people with respect.

Be on time.

Don't miss rehearsals. The only excuse for missing a rehearsal is death—your own.

Come to rehearsal prepared to work. (That is wear appropriate clothing, be physically and vocally warmed up, and have all personal props with you.)

Walk around the stage before each rehearsal and performance to check for any changes or safety hazards.

Do not do anything that could cause serious or permanent physical or emotional harm to yourself or any other actor or crew member. No show is more important than ensuring everyone's safety and well-being.

Never eat, drink, or smoke in costume, unless you have the director's and designer's permission.

Do not play music or turn on the television backstage or in the dressing rooms unless all actors agree to it. Make sure it is not so loud that you or others cannot hear time calls.

Always acknowledge time calls with a thank you or other appropriate response.

Do not disturb other actors twenty minutes before their first entrance. They may be preparing.

Never argue with the director or stage managers in public. Discussions should be held in private.

Always try anything the director asks you to do, unless it is unsafe.

Take care of your props and costumes; you are responsible for their care. Before each performance, make sure they are in their proper place and in working order, and put them back in their proper places after using them.

Never direct or give suggestions to other actors. Talk to the director or stage manager about all concerns.

Bring a pencil and paper to all rehearsals.

Write down all notes and work on them.

Work on lines and character outside rehearsal at least as many hours as during rehearsal.

Attend and participate in all strikes. (Unless it is not allowed by your union or theatre company.)

Consider giving cast cards or a small gift to the technical director, stage manager, director, and any appropriate crew people and designers at the last performance. In most theatres, it is a tradition.

Never alter your appearance with such changes as a hair cut, more or less facial hair, a new hair color, or tattoo without the director's and/or the costume designer's permission.

Report all safety concerns to the stage manager.

Don't borrow or use any other actor's make-up, sponges, or personal items without permission.

Don't gossip and don't listen to gossip.

STAYING ALIVE AND IN THE MOMENT
Active Listening and Watching

Acting is a combination of acting—doing things to the other character or actor—and reacting—staying open and responsive to what is being done to you. In order to be able to react, you must actively listen and watch what is happening to you and what is going on around you. All of your senses must be alive and on full alert. Your concentration must be on how the other person is reacting to what you are doing to them and on what you are receiving from them.

Ideally, after a good scene or exercise you should have a pretty good idea about what you just did, but you should also have a very, very clear idea of what the others did and how they reacted. This puts you in the moment and makes you alive in the scene. Staying alive in a scene gives you the illusion that it is the first time you are hearing the lines spoken to you, and it is the first time you are reacting to these lines or actions. This illusion can be achieved by listening and watching for any changes or subtleties. This way you are hearing the lines for the first time.

Playing Tennis

My favorite metaphor for acting is the game of tennis. In tennis, you do not say, "Okay, on this serve I am going to hit the ball in that corner and then you hit the ball back to me here, next to the net." That would be a very boring game—not really a game at all.

In tennis, you don't know where the ball will be. You stay alive and react to wherever it goes; sometimes you hit it . . . sometimes you miss it.

But you said you were going to hit it in this corner.

A scene should be just like a good tennis game. You stay alert and try to deliver your lines in relation to how someone else's lines are delivered to you. If the delivery is soft, you react to that. If the delivery is hard, you react to that. If the delivery is as you expected, you react to that. If it a total surprise, so much the better.

The Old Mirror Exercise

An oldie, but a goodie.

Face your partner. One person begins a slow movement. The other person copies that movement exactly. Use slow movements and your entire body. Proceed from movement to movement, letting them evolve. Work with your partner and try to move exactly as your partner does. This takes time and your full attention.

Rhythm and Pace Exercise

With your partner, decide who will be named A and who will be B. Begin a simple mirror exercise. This exercise should lead into one simple activity that becomes repetitive. That simple repetitive activity should continue for at least two minutes. After two minutes, A doubles the pace of the repetitive activity. B stays at the same pace for another thirty seconds.

Now, B slows down to half the speed of the original repetitions. A doubles the speed again and B decreases the speed by half again. Keep at those speeds for at least one minute. Now, reverse the process: A begins to slow down and B speeds up. Go back and forth several times.

 ## Ah, Ah, Ah, or The Nonsequitur Game

Tell your partner a story of something that happened the day before. After a few minutes, hesitate and say, "Ah, ah, ah." The partner immediately comes in and finishes the sentence. No matter what your partner says, you agree and continue the story following the premise or fact that your partner supplies. You and your partner can take turns trying to have a natural conversation, but each of you should occasionally hesitate with an "Ah, ah, ah," to which your partner should respond by finishing the line of thought.

 ## Repetition Exercise

You and your partner face each other. One person scans and comments on the other person's appearance. The other person simply agrees with the statement. For example:

You are beautiful.

Yes, I'm beautiful.

PARTNER A: You are wearing a blue shirt.

PARTNER B: Yes, I am wearing a blue shirt.

PARTNER A: You have brown hair.

PARTNER B: Yes, I have brown hair.

PARTNER A: You have a small scar on your cheek.

PARTNER B: Yes, I have a small scar.

This exercise should last at least five minutes, at which time partners should switch roles (B comments on A).

Repetition Exercise with a Twist

Do the repetition exercise, but this time the attitude, tone of voice, and body language of B can convey conflict or disagreement. Do not only comment on appearance but pick up on attitudes, emotions, etc. This can lead to an interesting, emotionally charged interchange. For example:

A: You look tired.

B: Yes, I look tired.

A: You don't think you look tired?

B: Yes, I don't think I look tired.

A: You don't like this exercise?

B: Yes, I don't like this exercise.

A: You don't like me to criticize you?

B: Yes, I don't like you to criticize me.

A: You think I'm very wrong about you being tired looking

B: Yes, I think you are very wrong about my being tired looking.

Eavesdropping Scene Exercise

You and your partner go someplace where people gather. Try to get as close to two people having a conversation as safely possible. Now, either using a tape recorder or taking quick notes, try to get at least one minute of their conversation. Leave and write down the conversation as best you can. As you are working, consider these questions:

• What was their relationship?

- What did they need from each other?
- How did the environment influence them?

Memorize the lines and perform the conversation on video-tape or for your class.

CONNECTING

Most scenes and exercises are interactions between people. To make those interactions seem real so as to entice and interest the audience, there must be a deep connection between the actors on stage. The words and movements of each actor must hit home in the other actors.

This comes, of course, from actively listening, watching, and believing what your partner is saying. Equally, it comes from the actor trying to be heard, seen, and believed by the other actors in the scene.

As in real life, some actors will naturally connect with certain people. With other actors, it may take more effort to connect on stage. However, it is one of the actor's most essential tasks. The actor must constantly keep working and concentrating on keeping or making a connection with the other people in the scene. One of the ways to do this is to talk to the other actor, not at him or her.

Connection Monologue Exercise

Both you and your partner write a small speech that begins with: "There is something I have never told anyone before." The speech should be twenty to forty words long, and its subject can be from either your lives or imagination. Memorize the speech. Then, sit facing each other and take turns delivering your speeches. The purpose of the exercise is for you to connect with your partner, so you each should concentrate on your partner to get him or her to hear, understand, and believe you.

Best/Worst Exercise

Many times you will have a scene in which you may not like your partner or a scene in which you have to despise your partner even though offstage the two of you are friends. The point of this exercise is to find something to always like or dislike about your partner. This is totally private work, you never tell the other person what you are thinking.

Face your partner. Each of you should try to memorize everything about the other person. Turn away. Try to imagine how the other person looks. Now decide the one thing that is worst about that person's appearance. Turn and look at that person again—don't stare at what you have decided is the worst thing. Let that "worst thing" take over, and now only see that "thing." When you think of this person, let that "worst thing" symbolize their whole presence. Turn away. Let the "worst thing" go—forget it for now.

Once again, imagine what the other person looks like. This time pick out the "best thing" about the other person. Turn back and look at that person again—don't stare at what you have decided is the "best thing." Let that "best thing" take over. Now let this thing symbolize your partner. Turn away and let this go for now, but remember it for future use.

STAGE FRIGHT

If you have stage fright, you are not alone. Almost everyone suffers from stage fright to some extent. In all the polls I have ever read about fears and anxiety, the number one fear is having to be in front of a group or audience. Here are a few ways that you can deal with it.

1. Get used to it.

   Without question, the best way to control stage fright is to not make it anything that is unusual. You do that by performing as much as possible. Get used to being on stage. Make it

like home. Take acting classes, do lots of scene work, volunteer to read aloud, do anything to get up and perform.

2. *Be prepared.*

   Even after years of acting and maintaining a basic control of stage fright, most actors will say they still feel uneasy or scared to death if they are underrehearsed. If you have done your work, you know what you are doing and where to move, and saying the lines becomes second nature, so that you can even get to the point of relaxing and having fun while you perform.

3. *Forget about it.*

   Hundreds of times I have heard actors say, "I was so scared I didn't think I could go on, but once I was out there, I was fine." This loss of fear came about because each actor's concentration went from focusing inward to focusing outward. Each of them stopped thinking about themselves and how they were feeling, and started focusing on what they had to do and what was happening in the world of the play. An actor's concentration should always be directed primarily outward. This outward focus is liberating and natural. It keeps you so busy you forget about your fears.

4. *Go with it.*

   There is a very interesting and helpful exercise that people with anxiety disorders and panic attacks are told to do by psychiatrists and other doctors. It is simply this directive: relish your fright. Say to yourself, "Man, I'm scared! No one has ever been more scared than I am. This is the worst. I'm probably going to pass out or die. I am so afraid. Not only that, I even hope I get even *more* frightened!" Often, this acceptance and exaggeration of your fear can help you diminish or even eliminate your anxiety. It may even help some people start to laugh and laughter can be a real tonic for fear.

5. *Get physical.*

   Sometimes good old physical exercise can dissipate the adrenaline that's thwarting your desire to perform. Shake, stretch, jog, or do a full warm-up to help get rid of your jitters, like the seven-minute physical and vocal warm-up described in Chapter 1.

6. *Just relax.*

   There are many relaxation exercises, meditations, or prayers that can calm you down and teach you to focus. There are even relaxation tapes that you can purchase or borrow from the library that can be very helpful for especially tense or fearful times.

7. *Breathe.*

   Just before you go on, put your concentration on your breath. Do slow controlled breathing from your diaphragm.

8. *It just doesn't matter.*

   Just before you go on, chant, "It just doesn't matter, it just doesn't matter, it's only a play. It won't stop war or cure cancer." In other words: play. Have fun!

 ## Clues Exercise

This is a fun party game that works wonders in getting people on stage with minimum stage fright. Divide the group into two teams, an A team and a B team. Each person writes down the titles or names of at least ten films, books, television shows, and famous people. The A team places their names in the B team's bowl. The B team puts their names in the A team bowl. Each person comes up on stage, picks a list of names, and is given one minute to give clues to the identity of as many people or titles on the list as they can. Only their own team tries to guess the answers. Any clue is acceptable except proper names. For each person or title identified, the team gets a point. The team with the most points wins.

MEMORIZATION

Anyone who has ever been in a play has heard some well-meaning friend or relative say "How did you ever learn all those lines?" Here are a few tips on how to learn all those lines.

1. *Just do it.*

   Say to yourself: "This is just part of my job. My job is to get the lines down as quickly and as thoroughly as possible so I can start the real interpretation work and can be free in rehearsal." Park your behind in a chair and just do it! Don't procrastinate. Now is the best time. This is the basic part of your craft. Just as an artist mixes his paints or stretches his canvas or a dancer stretches and warms up, you memorize.

I thought memorizing lines would be much harder.

2. *Don't bite off more than you can chew.*

   The biggest mistake most people make is to memorize too much at one sitting. Pick a small, realistic amount for each session. Stick with that amount to learn. It is better to really learn a small amount than to only partly learn a lot.

3. *Make it enjoyable.*

   Don't lock yourself up in a dark room and act as though memorization is a punishment. Try to make it enjoyable. Go to a park, the beach, or someplace with a view. Set yourself up in a place that is just yours and that is relaxing and comfortable. Give yourself rewards: Eat a piece of candy, listen to music from a new CD, do whatever can to make memorization more enjoyable.

4. *Know what you are saying.*

   Never memorize lines as though they have no meaning, like a child memorizing *The Pledge of Allegiance.* Find out the goal or need of each line. Ask yourself, "What does this character want to get from saying this line?" Once you understand why your character is saying this line, the line will have more meaning and will be more likely to stay in your memory.

5. *Write it out.*

   One trick some actors use to memorize lines is writing them out. There is something about the physical activity of writing the lines that cements them in some people's minds.

6. *Give it a tune.*

   Hard or tricky lines can be given a melody. Some people find learning a song easier than learning straight lines.

7. *Make it personal.*

   You've read it before, but this is the most important step in memorization: Make each image in each line personal. Have good, clear, personal images associated with your lines and you will be able to remember them almost automatically.

🎭 Stomp Exercise

This exercise explores physicality. Somehow it integrates the voice, mind, and body and can aid in memorization. It is also a good physical warm-up. I am not sure why the exercise works so well, but it does.

Take any speech or line you are beginning to memorize. Stand someplace soft, such as on a mat or on grass. Go through each word of each line. Stomp out each word. Try different levels of intensity. Stomp and jump up and down. Don't overdo it, however. It is possible to injure yourself in this exercise.

THINGS YOU CAN DO TO BECOME A BETTER ACTOR

1. *Get in the best physical shape you can.*

   Acting is a physical activity. It takes great stamina and energy. Playing a difficult leading role requires probably more energy than running a 10K race or playing a 90-minute soccer game.

   Exercise daily. Do a combination of aerobic and flexibility exercises. Also, watch what you eat. Actors must always train like athletes.

2. *Don't smoke.*

   Smoking robs you of breath. Breath is the actor's ammunition. Smoking also robs you of energy and can damage your voice.

3. *Don't take illegal or unprescribed drugs*

   Drugs do the opposite of what you as an actor are trying to do: They numb your emotions and perception. Drugs can also rob you of your health, energy, and control.

4. *Read and be curious.*

   Learn as much as you can about the world around you. The greatest actors and artists are all people blessed with a burning curiosity. Take courses on history, literature, psychology, or anything else that interests you. Travel. Experience all types of people. Stay open and active.

5. *Read aloud.*

   Every day read aloud. Get used to the sound of your own voice reading. Read signs as you walk or drive along. As you are doing recreational reading or homework, read part of it aloud.

6. *Watch great acting.*

   Never miss an opportunity to watch and study great actors. See as many live plays as possible.

   Rent classic films with great actors and watch the actors over and over again. Study their performances. Analyze why these particular performances stand out.

7. *Watch people.*

   Every day sit quietly and observe people. Give yourself small daily assignments during your observation. For example: watch body movement, how people walk, or how people make eye contact.

8. *Read a play a week.*

   If you read only one play a week, in two years you will have read over a hundred plays and will have a pretty good start on a great understanding and appreciation of dramatic literature. Most plays take less than two hours to read. Read a balance of the classics and contemporary plays.

9. *Keep a journal.*

   People who keep a journal or diaries have a rich source of past life experiences upon which to draw. Keeping a journal is also a great way to analyze your experiences. You can keep notes, secrets, things you observe, anything you want in your journal.

10. *Don't limit your look.*

    The best look for an actor is a rather neutral appearance. Too long, too short, or strangely dyed hair will limit you. Tattoos and body piercings can also limit you. You want to speak through your personality and the character you are playing, not through how you look. Personal ornamentation can limit your ability to do that and can affect your chances at being cast.

11. *Don't limit yourself.*

    The worst thing any artist can do is say, "I don't do that" or "I don't want to be with those type of people." Unless it is immoral, illegal, or dangerous, be willing to undergo new and very different experiences. This can only make you grow as an artist.

12. *Take singing lessons.*

    Whether or not you ever sing a note on stage, singing lessons can be of great help to an actor. They teach you dynamics, control, tone, and vocal musicality. All of these abilities are of great use to an actor. Also, take dance, yoga, tai chi, and martial arts classes. They help you become aware of your body and help you increase flexibility.

13. *Direct.*

    I have heard dozens of actors say that they never really learned how to act until they started directing. Directing forces you to organize your own acting methods and to become objective.

14. *Be honest with yourself.*

    Be aware of your strengths and limitations. Occasionally take stock of your skills and what you look like. Decide what it is you need to improve upon or just accept what you consider shortcomings.

15. *Write.*

Write screenplays, plays, and scenes. The actors who get the most work are the ones who come up with their own projects.

16. *Never stop learning.*

Keep taking acting classes, learning new skills, and generally just growing as a human being. The worst thing that can happen is for an actor to think they know enough.

17. *Don't be a jerk.*

You'll last a lot longer and get cast more often if you are nice to people.

ACTING TOOLS (*THE TIONS*)

The following terms define the main tools and abilities you need in rehearsals and performance. They all end in *tion*. So for fun I call them *the tions*.

Attention

Attention can be described as the act of directing your senses to what you hear, see, taste, feel, and smell. In an improv, an exercise, or a scene, you should see yourself in the middle of all the action. You are receiving lots of stimuli, analyzing that stimuli, and reacting to it. Using your attention, you are staying alive, aware, and open.

There are a number of benefits to properly using your attention. One of the benefits is that it gives you focus. You are "in the moment" and thus the moment is real to you. Properly using your attention is also the most successful way to dispel stage fright. If you are focusing on the "universe" around you, you *do not* have the time or ability to be self-conscious, and it is self-consciousness that most often causes stage fright.

Often we use our attention just to get along in the real world. Most people rarely go through the day totally self-absorbed, just concentrating on themselves. More likely they are in a rather open state, actively absorbing and reacting to the world around them. This should be your goal as an actor: Stay open, actively open in the sense that you are intensely absorbing, analyzing, and reacting to everything around you.

Competition

Relationships, especially dramatic relationships, are like games. All parties involved in the game want to win. In a dramatic relationship, all the characters must compete to achieve their goals. The stronger you as a character compete with all the other characters to win your goals in a scene, the more engaging the scene becomes. You as an actor and you as the character must always strive and expect to win every scene. When you win, it is important to see and feel that sense of victory—it gives joy to the scene. When you lose, it is also important to feel and acknowledge the frustration. This gives tension to a scene and provides the motivation for the next attempt at achieving victory.

— *Always feel and acknowledge the wins!* —

— *Always feel and acknowledge the losses!* —

Never let the resolution of a goal trail off as if it didn't matter; it does matter, and how strongly you react defines our interest in you as a person and a dramatic character.

Concentration

Your job as an actor is to concentrate and live in the dramatic universe created in a scene. The other, "outside universe" is just that:

outside. You have a choice of one of two techniques to create the dramatic universe on which you must concentrate. You can either:

1. Ignore all outside stimuli, like the audience, the usher bringing people down the aisle to watch the first scene, and the fat sound man smoking the cigar about ten feet from where you are seated. Put your full and total concentration on the area that is specifically created for this scene.

or

2. Incorporate everything, including the "outside universe," into this strange universe. In your weird consciousness, there just happens to be an audience watching—complete with rude ushers—and sometimes there is a smelly, fat sound man just in the corner of your eye. This is just how the Salvador Dali–Alice in Wonderland world happens to be.

Believe it or not, both techniques can work.

Should you ignore or incorporate? A lot depends on your unique personality and sometimes on the type of scene on which you are working. With more intimate scenes the ignoring technique might work better. With more expansive and outgoing scenes, the incorporating technique might work best. Either way, using these techniques will give a certain quality and texture to your scene.

Expectation

Acting for the most part takes place with the very next moment in mind, so that you are always expecting something to happen. Characters expect to win. Even if they are in an impossible situation, they always have that hope, that desire, that expectation that things are going to work out somehow. You keep going for it. A character that does not struggle or expect to finally come out on the top is a character that the audience will not care about or give its attention. The struggle and the expectation of the character gives the character a reason for being in the play or film.

The play *The Three Sisters* by Anton Chekhov should never be about three sisters who want desperately to go to Moscow but never get to go and never really think or hope they will go. It is a play about three sisters who know they *will* go to Moscow. Up to the last minute of the play, they expect to go to Moscow. Even after the play is over, we should have the feeling they will continue to struggle and expect to finally get there. Struggle and expectation gives your character a soul and a compelling energy.

Imagination

There is no greater gift for an actor to have than a great imagination. Some people are naturally gifted with a powerful imagination all their lives. Others somehow lose this gift as they become adults. If you think you need to rediscover your imagination, it is still very possible. As the character Bagger Vance, from the Steven Pressfield novel and Robert Redford film *The Legend of Bagger Vance*, says, "You just gotta go find it."

How to Cultivate Your Imagination

1. Get over yourself. Stop being too old and mature to play, daydream, and make believe.
2. Take time out of every day to daydream.
3. Watch people. Imagine their life stories.
4. Go places. Invent stories about this place. What was it like a hundred years ago, a hundred years from now?

A good actor must be like a child: always playing, always inventing, and always using the imagination.

Intuition and Inspiration

I have heard from a number of actors, "Boy I don't know what happened tonight. I just felt inspired. I just intuitively knew what to do." I have felt this inspiration and intuition myself. This is a wonderful feeling and there is no denying that those moments happen on stage and in front of the camera. Inspiration and intuitive action come because you are prepared. You know the situation completely and you are living in the moment. They happen because you are ready for them to happen. You are in control enough to lose control and stay open and ready to react.

Observation

There are two very important levels of observation for you as an actor. The first level requires that you simply stay aware in your everyday life. You should always be alert for things you can bring to your characters. Actively watch mannerisms, gestures, body language, emotional outbursts, physical quirks, and vocal phrasing in other people. The other people of the world are a great resource for you. When you see things of interest or that you may be able to use, make mental notes or even write them in your journal.

The next level of observation occurs during a rehearsal or a performance. When you are on the set, stay as aware and flexible as possible.

— *Watch, listen, and react.* —

— *Stay alive. Stay aware.* —

Personalization

Everything the playwright writes must transform from his or her thoughts to your thoughts. You can make this transformation by making the playwright's thoughts personal. By the second or third reading of a scene, you must start to take ownership of the words. Substitute experiences and desires from your life with those in the play to help bring the lines to life for you. Take your time. Look for clear, rich, and emotionally charged mental images. The more real and alive these images and thoughts are for you, the more alive and real they will be for the people listening to you.

Relaxation

Perhaps the most difficult thing to finally learn as an actor is how to be as comfortable on stage, or in front of a camera, as you are in regular, unobserved life. The ability to relax in these situations is the full measured difference between a beginning and a seasoned, skilled actor.

Ways to relax:

1. Become familiar with your craft. The more you act and the more you are in front of people, the more natural performing should become.

2. Have strong goals and strive for them. If you are engaged, your self-consciousness will tend to disappear.

3. Be involved in the environment. Through your imagination, believe you are in the environment of the scene. This will help the "outside world" disappear.

4. Connect with your partner. Really watch and listen and you will become engaged and relaxed.

5. Breathe and get physically active. Purposely slow and control your breath. Relax your muscles and let your tension flow away from you. Get physical before and during a scene (if appropriate).

6. Have fun! Acting is supposed to be fun. Be silly. Chant just before you enter:

> It just doesn't matter.
> It just doesn't matter.
> It's only acting.
> It's not brain surgery
> or a tax audit.
> It's acting.
> It's playing.
> It's make believe.

Situation

Situation is everything, absolutely everything, the character and actor need to know about the character's dramatic universe that may have an effect on that character. To this end, the most important phrase in an actor's arsenal is: *Be specific*. Be specific in everything you explore and know about your character's situation. There should never be any "Sort ofs," "Kindas," or "I Thinks." Know! Be certain. Don't guess when it comes to a situation. Knowing as much as you can about a situation will make it real to you, your partner, and the audience.

Well, ah, ah, I guess, uh, I'm sorta, kinda...
Well, I never really thought about it before.

Visualization

Visualization is the attempt and ability to imagine experiences before they happen. It has been a successful exercise that has been used by Olympic athletes for many years. Gymnasts, pole vaulters,

divers, and others try to visualize their routine or next attempt. This visualization helps them both mentally and physically prepare.

Visualization can be a useful preparation exercise for actors. Sit at home and visualize yourself on the set going through your action. Sit in the audience section or off set and visualize yourself in the next scene. Walk the set. As you move around, visualize yourself and the other players going through the various movements and actions.

3

Getting Yourself Going and Your Creative Juices Flowing

IMPROVISATION: WORKING WITHOUT A NET

Improvisation, or working without a written script, offers great opportunities and even greater challenges for the actor. There are opportunities with improvisation because you have almost no limitations. You can draw upon the whole world and your wonderfully vivid imagination to create situations. You are free to experiment, discover new things, and be as creative as you wish.

The challenges of working without a script are that you must be very spontaneous. You must be aware of everything around you and be able to acutely listen, watch, and work with your partner(s). Finally, you must always be prepared for surprises.

Rules of Engagement

There are a number of things you need to know to successfully improvise:

1. Never deny, block, or argue with your partner. *Denying* is not going along with your partner. For instance, if your partner says, "Well, here we are at the North Pole," you don't say, "No, we're on Fifth Avenue in New York City." *Blocking* is very much like denying, but not as obvious. It happens when one partner starts to build a situation and the other partner doesn't help develop that situation, or worse yet, detours from the situa-

tion that the first person is trying to establish. *Arguing* is just what it sounds like: Two characters improv a scene in which they have a disagreement. This is usually boring and goes nowhere.

2. Never go for the laugh. Go for the reality of the situation.

3. Establish a relationship with your partner right away. Improvs about strangers rarely work; they are most successful when they concern two characters discovering each other.

4. Establish and use the environment around the characters.

5. Don't worry about time constraints. Just work in the moment.

6. Don't worry about having a beginning, middle, or ending to your improv. Work instead to make each moment as full and real as possible.

7. Consider doing your improv with a specific goal in mind, such as exploring character, relationships, your environment, or a physical eccentricity, like an exaggerated limp or a strong accent. When improvs are performed with such specific goals, keep them simple by just concentrating on the one goal.

8. Listen, watch, and connect with your partner(s). This is not a competition, so you should work with, never against, your partner.

Here are a few exercises that explore improvisation. They explore being in the moment, active watching and listening, creating the illusion of the first time something is done, giving goals importance, and acknowledging winning.

Garage Sale Improvisation

Have a garage sale, using lots of props as items for sale. Individuals and partners visit the garage sale with specific needs or with an agenda. Practice creating conflict through the situation. Here's a few examples of situations that can lead to conflict:

- One person thinks something that belongs to them is being sold.
- Neighbors want you to stop your garage sale because it is bringing in riffraff and causing parking problems.
- A visitor thinks the garage-sale items are too expensive.
- An official tells you a permit is needed to have a garage sale.
- Two groups find something they must have or secretly believe is very valuable.

Last Line Improvisation

You and your partner work with another couple. Imagine you are all in a restaurant. Each pair sits at a different table in the restaurant and has a specific relationship and agenda (i.e., one couple is having a business lunch during which one of them is being fired, and the other couple is in the middle of a marriage proposal).

Start an improv with your partner for about a minute, then suddenly stop. Whatever the last line was in your improv becomes the first line of the other couple. Go back and forth several times. Each time, the duration of each improv becomes shorter.

Simple Partner Improvisation

You and your partner stand on stage. Ask the audience to determine a place, a time, the relationship between you and your partner, what you and your partner need from each other, and what problem you two have to overcome. With these five elements in mind, briefly plan with your partner how to start an improv and consider where you might end up. Then, start the improv, work with each other, and let happen whatever comes up.

Newspaper Improvisation

With your partner, find a story in the news section of a newspaper. Using that story, develop an improvisation using the "who, what, and where" of that news story. Just use this as a starting point. You can build on the story if you want.

 ## Two Minutes From Yesterday Exercise

Within reason, try to physically re-create everything you did the first two minutes you got home yesterday after school or work. Use props. Set up the stage or classroom to as closly as possible resemble your room or living room. Don't perform. Keep conversation to a minimum and just try to remember and physically re-create those two minutes.

Now, adding imagined circumstances, do the same exercise with the exact same actions. Don't consciously change any of your actions, but imagine:

- You have just won the lottery.
- You were just fired.
- You just had a great date.
- You have the stomach flu.
- You are caught in a blizzard.
- It is 105 degrees both inside and outside.
- It is 105 degrees outside, but 60 degrees inside.

Afterward, note how your actions were changed by these new situations.

 ## Apartment Complex Exercise

Place chairs in groups of twos and threes on stage. Split the class in half. One half performs and the other half acts as the audience.

Place actors in groups of twos and threes in the chairs. Give each group a number and a place in which to imagine themselves in an apartment complex, such as in an apartment, a whirlpool, or the weight room. Either give them a relationship and situation or let them determine their own. Each group may speak only when their number is called out. Occasionally, different groups may interact.

Airport Waiting Room Exercise

This exercise is a variation of the apartment complex exercise, except that it takes place in an airport waiting room where people are waitng for an overdue airplane. This time, the second half of the class performs for the group that performed during the apartment complex exercise.

Deep Impact Exercise

This exercise is named after the disaster movie in which an asteroid is speeding toward Earth. For this exercise, you and your partner work with a larger group.

Imagine that only a few people can be saved in the impending disaster. These people will go into deep shelters created by the government. You and your partner talk for ten or fifteen minutes. Find out as much about each other as possible in that time. Return to the group, present that information, and plead for your partner to be included in the select few.

Be Your Partner Exercise

You and your partner talk and take notes on each other's life. Ask questions about each other, such as questions on each of your likes and dislikes, goals, past experiences, past or present jobs, relationships, and secrets. Return to the group and introduce your partner in the first person. In other words, take on your partner's identity. Try to capture the essence of your partner's movement and posture.

 ## Truth and Lie Exercise

Form a circle or other formation with a group so that everyone can see everyone else. Each person takes a turn telling two personal stories. One of the stories must be true, the other story must be a lie. Go all the way around the group, then have the group decide which story from each person is true.

 ## Lost and Found Exercise

You and a partner enter a room. You have lost something. You search everywhere and finally find it.

Do this three or four times. Each time, the object changes in importance to you. Explore the range from slight annoyance at not finding the object to facing a life-and-death situation.

OPEN SCENES

Open or contentless scenes are those in which the actor has been given almost no information. These scenes offer great opportunities for the actor to make choices, be creative, and start thinking in specifics.

To get the most out of these scenes, the actors should fill in as much detail as possible about a scene, characters, situations, and environments. Each scene must have the following: a place, a time, a relationship that is understood or established, and a situation to handle or a problem to solve.

Open Scene #1

A: Yes

B: No

A: Yes

B: No

A: Yes

B: No

A: Yes

B: No

A: Yes

B: Maybe

A: Maybe

B: Maybe

A: No

B: No

A: No

B: No

Open Scene #2

A: Yes

B: Yes

A: I can't believe it

B: Oh, yes

A: It

B: It must be

A: This is wonderful

B: You think so

A: Don't you

B: Well

A: Oh

B: Oh

A: Well

B: Well

A: Who would have guessed

B: That is true

A: I can't believe it

B: Oh yes

A: Yes

B: No

 ## Open Scene #3

In this open scene, an actor can either trail off or begin to fill in the sentence endings. The other actor should interrupt.

A: Is it. . . ?

B: Are you. . . ?

A: Didn't you. . . ?

B: Could it be. . . ?

A: Should we. . . ?

B: Wasn't it only. . . ?

A: Wasn't it more like. . . ?

B: Could it have been. . . ?

A: Wouldn't it have been. . . ?

B: Do you still. . . ?

A: Would you like to. . . ?

B: Wouldn't it be nice. . . ?

A: Wouldn't it though. . . ?

B: Wouldn't it. . . ?

A: Would it. . . ?

B: No I don't think so. . . ?

 ## Open Scene #4

This open scene is based on a scene from *The Three Sisters* by Anton Chekhov.

A: I'm glad they are leaving

B: That's understandable

A: I'll be right back

B: Are you going somewhere?

A: I'll be right back

B: What happened yesterday

A: Do you love me

B: You look upset

A: Please say something

B: What

A: Anything. Something

B: Don't

A: Something. I'm going

B: I'm going with you

A: No no don't

B: What

A: I haven't had any coffee today. Have someone make me some

 ## Open Scene #5

This is based on *The Cherry Orchard* by Chekhov.

A: I can't find it

B: What

A: I can't find it

B: What are you looking for

A: I packed it myself

B: Where are you going

A: Away

B: Far

A: Enough

B: Oh

A: Where could I have put it

B: It's cold outside

A: Really I haven't looked

B: Nothing will ever be the same

A: No nothing

 **Open Scene #6**

Decisions

A: What do you want to do?

B: What do you want to do?

A: I don't know. What do you want to do?

B: I don't know.

A: Me either. You decide.

B: You decide.

A: You.

B: You.

A: We could go to the place.

B: We went there last time.

A: That's right. I forgot.

B: We could go to the other place.

A: We always go there.

B: I know.

A: Think.

B: You think.

A: I always think.

B: Right.

A: What do you want to do?

B: What do you want to do?

 Open Scene #7

Conflict

A: I want it

B: You can't have it

A: I need it

B: I need it

A: No

B: Yes

A: I deserve it

B: So what

A: It's not fair

B: Life isn't fair

A: I'm going to get it

B: Just try

A: I will

B: You will lose

A: Oh yeah

B: Yeah

A: You wait and see

B: You wait and see

A: I want it

B: You can't have it

 ## Open Scene #8

Decision

A: I'm going

B: Go

A: I'm going

B: Go

A: Do you want to go with me

B: Go with you

A: Go with me

B: Go with you

A: Go with me

B: You

A: Yes

B: Let me think

A: Well

B: Well what

A: Forget it

B: That is easy for you to say

A: No it isn't

B: Oh yes it is

 ## Open Scene #9

Cut Off and Trailing

A: That makes me so. . .

B: I know it makes me so. . .

A: I can see that it. . .

B: I know that you. . .

A: It really, really

B: Really, really

A: The only thing to do is. . .

B: I suppose we could. . .

A: But. . .

B: But. . .

A: That makes me so. . .

B: I know it makes me. . .

A: Oh well

B: Oh well

 ## Open Scene #10

A: Ooh

B: Ooh

A: Huh

B: Himmm

A: Mmm

B: Ha

A: Ha ha

B: Hey

A: Yeah

B: Naw

A: Ooh ooh ooh ooh ooh

B: Mmm mmm mmm mmm

A: Uuh

B: Uuh

4

Exploring the Script and Scene

GOALS

Giving the Lines Direction

Let's define these words first:

Action: Anything done or said by an actor/character in a scene.

Motivation: The act, situation, or experience that instigates a reaction or action.

Goals, intentions, and objectives: All three words mean the same thing: The final desired outcome of an action. I prefer to use the word *goal* because it is short and simple, and it seems more game oriented. Human interactions and action are very often types of games.

Motivation vs. goal: It is very important to know the motivation for any action, as in "what started all this?" It is much more important, however, for the actor to understand what the character wants to achieve through a particular action. This is the goal. The goal is always in the future. Acting is about actions in the moment that progress toward the foreseeable future.

Goals are always positive. This means that goal-oriented actions are always carried out with the idea of improving a situation or the condition of the character. It is not possible to achieve a negative goal. Goals are also selfish endeavors. Through them, a

character seeks to better the situation or condition of himself or herself, often at the expense of the other persons in the scene. Take, for example, the villain-with-the-damsel-on-the-tracks scenario.

Don't worry, this won't hurt (me) a bit.

Here, the villain carries out goals that are positive for himself by placing the dainty damsel on the railroad tracks. By getting rid of her, he hopes to at last get control of the mortgage on the damsel's ranch. This will give him property, money, and power, thus bettering his present condition, which he considers to be a very positive goal, at the expense of the damsel's life.

Goal Levels

There are several levels and types of goals. These goals go from the general to the very specific, even to the question of developing individual line and phrase goals.

1. *The ultimate goal.*

   Every character in every play or film has the same ultimate goal: To live happily ever after. Everything that character does works toward achieving this end.

2. *The main goal.*

   Each character has one overwhelming need or desire. This is the character's main goal. The main goal gives a spine, or structure, to a character. To find the main goal of a character, ask yourself what the character must do or achieve in order to live happily ever after.

3. *The immediate goal.*

   In order for your character to achieve his or her main goal, he or she must conquer or at least deal with many immediate goals. An immediate goal is what the character wants or needs in the moment. Knowing what your character needs at any given moment is your most important task as an actor. Your needs give life to your character.

   While developing and re-hearsing a character it is essential to always keep asking: "What do I need?" Then ask yourself again, "Is that what I really need? Is that what I really, really need?" Until you are completely satisfied with your answer, your work is incomplete.

   I need it!   You can't have it.

4. *Encounter goal (French scene goals).*

   In many French plays, scenes are broken down by entrances and exits. Each time a new character enters or leaves the stage, it is a new scene. Each time a character enters or leaves, thus changing the number of people interacting, there must be a slight change or shift in what each character wants from the remaining people in the scene. The entrance or exit changes the focus of the scene and creates or blocks opportunities for the other characters. So, as an actor you must ask yourself how another person's arrival or departure affects what you want or need to do.

5. *Action goals.*

   Each phrase or small line in a scene has an action goal. It is the desired effect of that phrase or line. Take a simple line like

"You are so nice." Depending on what you want to convey to the person to whom you are speaking, you will say that line with a certain inflection, force, and use of body language. What you have to do with that line to convey your intent or need is your action goal.

Now try saying "You are so nice," with a variety of different action goals: to tease, to threaten, to confuse, to seduce, to patronize, to warm, to destroy, to mother, and to comfort.

The way the line is conveyed changes dramatically with your need or action goal, and in this way action goals create action. The stronger, the more imaginative, and the more specific the goal, the more powerful and interesting the delivery of the line.

The Goal Order

1. You say your lines or do your action (action goals),
2. To get your immediate and/or encounter goals,
3. In order to achieve your main goal,
4. So you can succeed in attaining your ultimate goal.

Goals, Obstacles, and Conflicts

A story in which the main character or characters achieve all their goals easily, without struggle or grief, would be a very boring story. It would not be a dramatic story at all. Drama comes from the clash between a character's goals and the obstacles or conflicts that the character encounters.

Conflicts and obstacles are those things that keep a character from automatically or easily obtaining what he or she needs and wants. Obstacles are unfeeling, careless, sometimes benign things that are in a character's way. They can be things like rules, war, distance, mountain ranges, rivers, quick sand, giant rolling boulders, monsters, a lack of time, lack of strength, or lack of knowledge.

Conflicts generally come from opposing characters in a scene. They happen when two opposing character goals come into direct contact. One goal must eventually win and the other must eventually lose. This opposition produces dramatic struggle. The stronger, more important, or difficult an obstacle or conflict is, the more interesting the struggle. The audience typically identifies and roots for characters who must struggle to finally get what they want.

There are two approaches to developing and working with obstacles and conflicts.

1. *Supplied obstacle and conflict.*

   Most of the time, the playwright or script writer provides a character with the obstacles and conflicts necessary to create the dramatic struggle in a scene. It is then the actor's job to discover the relevance of those obstacles and conflicts to his or her character's goals and to work against them accordingly.

2. *Imagined or planted obstacles and conflicts.*

   If there are no apparent conflicts or obstacles, it then becomes the responsibility of the actor to find or create them. Without them, your character will tend to be boring and uninvolved in the situation. Use your imagination. Find interesting and unique reasons that identify why your character does not easily get what he or she wants.

— *Dramatic situation = Conflicts or obstacles opposing character goals* —

— *Easy is boring.* —

— Struggle is interesting —

— Drama is struggle —

Goals and Subtext

Subtext is usually defined as the thoughts you have as you are speaking a line or doing a physical action that affect that line or physical action. It is sometimes called your *inner monologue* or *inner dialogue*.

I suppose that in real life it is possible to be doing or saying one thing and completely thinking about something else. In fact, I believe my students do it most of the time. (Joke) In dramatic situations, however, I really can't see this ever happening. What the characters are thinking is always related to what they want or need: They are thinking about their goals, and they are thinking about the immediate future and what they have to do to make things better in that future. They are also thinking about the person with whom they are interacting and what they can do to or for that other person to get what they want. In a dramatic situation, subtext is directly related to a character's wants and needs.

— Subtext = Goals —

 ## Action Goal Exercise

Work with a series of simple lines like:

- I love you.
- Go away.
- You make me so mad.
- Who do you think you are?

Choose a strong action word, like *to hurt*. Get a thesaurus and find some synonyms for *to hurt*, such as: to injure, to wound, to distress, and to bruise. Explore how the images or feelings produced by these variations on *to hurt* change your delivery or action goal when you say those simple lines.

Now, try varied verb goals that are extremely different, like:

- To hurt
- To warm
- To madden
- To kill
- To annihilate
- To inspire
- To enslave

Finally, add movement to the exercise, such as a step or gesture.

 ## Main Goals Exercise

Try to remember characters from your favorite plays or films. What do you think their main goals are? First think of major characters, such as:

- Hamlet
- Stanley Kowalski
- Rhett Butler (*Gone with the Wind*)
- Jack (*Titanic*)
- Saint Joan
- Blanche DuBois
- E.T. (*E.T.*)

Think of smaller or more obscure characters, such as:

- The Mother in *Equus*
- The Father in *The Miracle Worker*
- Natasha in *Three Sisters*
- A Guard in *Julius Caesar*
- Mrs. Linde in *A Doll's House*

- The Messenger in *Oedipus Rex*
- *Goose* in *Top Gun*
- Jabba the Hut in *Star Wars*

Make your own list.

Active Watching Exercises

Become an active audience member. As you watch a play, film, or television show, pick out one or two characters. Ask yourself what the main, immediate, and encounter goals of those characters are.

Occasionally, try to dissect one line at a time. Ask what the actor/character is trying to achieve with that particular line.

Watch people. Daily, find a place where you can observe people. Try someplace like a shopping mall, a coffeehouse, the school cafeteria, an airport, or a hospital waiting room. Ask yourself what the people you see need from each other.

Look at that weirdo.

Simple Goal Action Circle Exercise

You and your classmates form a circle around your instructor. Your instructor should then give a simple line, such as "Get out of here," or "You are so cute," or "I'm warning you!" You and the class say the line.

Now, the instructor faces an individual and making eye contact asks him or her to deliver the line with one simple action goal. Some suggested action goals include:

- To warn
- To destroy
- To befriend
- To confuse
- To seduce
- To tease
- To hurt
- To thrill
- To inspire
- To patronize
- To belittle
- To kill
- To comfort

Simple Goal Action Circle with Physicalization

This is the same exercise as the "Simple Goal Action Circle," except that in this exercise you and your classmates should include a strong physical movement when you deliver a line, such as several quick steps or a large hand gesture. Make sure the movement supports the action goal.

IMAGES

Owning the Words: Saying Your Lines Like You Mean Them

Most actors speak lines as if they are reciting the *Pledge of Allegiance* or a memorized poem assigned to them by a sadistic seventh-grade teacher. The words do not seem to come from their own mind, imagination, or heart. It is as if they are borrowing the lines from the playwright and they must be careful not to break them.

You must own the lines. The lines must, somehow, transform from being words on a printed page into your own thoughts, images, and feelings. The lines following your character's name must become yours. You must come to believe that you own them, that they come from you, and that they have meaning and worth to you. Then, you must be determined to communicate that meaning and worth to the other characters in the world of the play or screenplay.

Make It Personal

The lines must somehow seem to come from your own personal life or imagination. This can be achieved by the use of clear, personalized images.

Let's say you have the following line: "I went to the beach today." When you deliver that line, do not think of some generic beach; make it a beach from your own life. Make it a beach that

means something to you. When you say the line, think about *that* beach. Try to make the people to whom you are speaking see *that* beach. Of course, your attempt to communicate your image of a beach won't succeed completely; other people will still have their own images of a beach. It is the trying to communicate your own clear image that will make it real for you and give the line meaning. When it becomes real for you, you will begin to own the words in the line.

Try using clear, personalized images with these lines:

Mary had a little lamb, his fleece was white as snow.

Out, out damned spot. Out I say.

To be or not to be, that is the question.

I went to the zoo today.

Don't you love ice cream.

Let's go.

Bored, bored, bored.

Connect with each line no matter how simple or complex. Find clear, personally loaded images for each phrase or important word. Do this on words and phrases you encounter throughout the day. Do it every time you begin working on a scene and you will see your acting immediately improve and become engaging.

Imaging Exercise #1

Find random nouns and verbs from a script. For each word, try to create clear, personal images (mind pictures). Use a mixture of concrete and abstract words. Examples:

Concrete	Abstract
Beach	Love
Zoo	Hope
Dog	Honor

Fire	God
Wound	Wisdom
Run	Fear
Flee	Respect
Drive	Hate
Home	Memory
Girlfriend	Heaven
Christmas	Faith
Vacation	Courage

Describe wha⟨...⟩n tape, or describe it to your class. ⟨...⟩t communicating the images to th⟨...⟩urself, finding very real personal an⟨...⟩s for each word.

Imaging

Choose several ⟨...⟩r song. Say the line aloud. By conjuring up your own ⟨...⟩cture, try to verbally paint what you see and how you feel about each line. The more real and emotionally loaded the phrase or word is for you, the more real it will be to the audience and the character or actor to whom you are speaking.

Imaging Exercise #3

Read aloud daily. Get used to your voice speaking written words. Read aloud whenever you get the opportunity. For example, read the information on the cereal box out loud as you are having breakfast. Make each word you speak mean something. Never rush through the words. If you are having breakfast with another person, try to make them really hear each word by using clear images.

 Imaging Exercise #4

Poems and Children's Stories

Find a group of children, senior citizens, or any other group.
Prepare and read aloud a very descriptive poem or children's story.
Make the words come alive to you and the group.

A Final Word about Images

As you prepare for a role, you must concentrate on creating images for each important word or phrase in your script. You must
do this in conjunction with discovering your goals. You must create
these images before you even begin memorization—in fact, it
makes memorization much easier. Your association of images with
words or phrases must be fairly concrete before you start major
rehearsals. You do not take time in actual rehearsal to search for
images. Sometimes new images will replace old images as you work.
You should stay flexible and allow this to happen during the rehearsal period.

PHYSICAL AND ENVIRONMENTAL INFLUENCES AND AWARENESS

Most acting scenes seem to take place in some perfect place; the temperature is just right, no one is eavesdropping on the scene, no one may interrupt you, etc.

— *Perfect places make boring acting places.* —

Physical and environmental influences can give texture and tension to a scene. By concentrating on environmental aspects of a scene, you help put your character in the scene. You can also help alleviate your self-consciousness and stage fright.

To more fully integrate physical and environmental influences into the scene, ask yourself as the character:

How do outside things influence, help, or threaten me?

Do I have enough time to complete everything I want to do?

How is my health and energy?

Am I safe here?

What time is it?

What is the temperature?

Take account of your senses:

What do I smell?

What do I feel?

What do I hear?

What do I taste?

What do I see (distances, shapes, people, colors, new and strange things)?

How am I influenced by what my five senses are detecting?

Consider where you are:

Do I like this place? Am I comfortable here, or. . . ?

How do other people feel about this place?

Is this place secure? Can people overhear what I am saying? Could someone walk in on us?

 ## Influences Exercise

Do an open scene. This time add strong physical influences, such as:

- Having a cold
- Being in pouring down rain
- Being in the middle of a heat wave
- Being on a crowded bus
- Being in a place with an awful smell
- Being in a wind storm
- Being near people who are listening
- Being sleep deprived
- Being starved
- Eating some great ice cream
- Looking for someone to rescue you
- Not being able to get comfortable

Come up with your own unique environmental and physical influences.

Be Aware of Everything around You

When you walk on stage or the set, take time to really look at it. Walk around. Touch things. If this is a place that you are supposed to know, take time to really know it. You are not a visitor here. You belong here. If this is a new place, for your character, take time to note those things that might interest or attract him or her.

Places have personalities. Get to know the personality of the place where you are going to act. Stages have very different personalities. Every actor worth his or her salt can get feelings from stages. There is always a great deal of energy, history, and magic in every stage. Take time to find it.

 ## Walking the Stage Exercise

The first thing you need to do every time you enter a stage or set is to walk it. You wander around. Look for changes, problems, or possible safety concerns. Just get reacquainted with this space. Before the rehearsal or performances is the time to find things out about this space. You do not want to be surprised while you are on stage or in front of the camera.

 ## Physical Joke Exercise

Choose a joke that is at least fifteen seconds long. Now, tell it in different imagined physical situations, such as:

- In a freezing snow storm
- As you are digging a ditch on a hot summer day
- While someone is eavesdropping
- On a very bumpy plane ride
- While you have the stomach flu
- As you are falling in love
- After you haven't slept in two days
- While there is an awful smell coming from somewhere
- On a beautiful spring day
- After you have had too much coffee

 ## Describe an Event Exercise

You and your partner are witnesses of an imagined major event, such as an accident, an explosion, a fight, or a contest. You and your partner make a cell phone call and describe the event, passing the phone back and forth, and being as specific as possible. Have a goal for making the phone call and being extremely descriptive.

 ## Describe a View Exercise

Imagine you are someplace with a great view. Describe what you see. Say, for example:

- Look at the man over there.
- Do you see that car?
- Isn't that tree beautiful!

Do it twice, the first time see things offstage right or left, the second time see them directly downstage, in the audience area or directly above the audience's head.

 ## Musical Speech Exercise

This exercise explores physicality and active listening.

Take any short, memorized speech of under thirty seconds. Prerecord ten different thirty-second bits of music or switch the radio to get different selections. Each selection of music should be very different from the preceding selection. For example, you might choose Mozart, Wagner, John Cage, country western, heavy metal, soft jazz, fusion jazz, punk, elevator muzak, or a children's song. Listen and let the music influence your delivery as you give your speech.

 ## Sound Effect Speech Exercise

Prerecord ten to fifteen sound effects. Try to find a wide variety of sound effects, such as:

- Bombs
- Waves
- Lightning

- Speeding cars
- Screams
- Rain
- Haunted house sounds
- Bells
- Children playing
- Applause

Memorize a short, fifteen-second speech. Let the various sounds influence your delivery.

RELATIONSHIPS

Scenes in theatre and film are usually about people needing things from each other. These desires can sometimes be very direct but often they are compli-cated and less than obvious. The following questions can help re-veal to an actor a character's true needs.

1. *What do I need from this person?* This should be asked during the first reading of the scene. It is asked from the character's point of view. Usually your first instincts about what the character needs are right.

2. *Why do I need it?* This is where it starts to get tricky. The answer to this ques-tion usually requires quite a bit more information. You must

know the whole play and be aware of the history of the characters' relationships and the desired future of your character.

3. *Is it easy or difficult to get what I need?*
   Boring scenes are scenes in which the characters get their goals too easily. If, for some reason, the playwright has not provided strong obstacles in a scene, you must find them. There are a number of places you can find such obstacles:

   In personality traits. You may be too shy or too proud. You may get panic attacks when in difficult situations or you may have no self-confidence.

   In situational circumstances. You may not know if you have enough time to do something or whether someone might walk in on you any minute. Or, you might not know the other person in the situation very well.

   In psychological problems. You might have severe anxiety. You might be paranoid about your situation, or you may think the other person in the situation is possessed with a demon.

   Any of these obstacles can give a new and intriguing dimension to a scene. Use your imagination. Come up with interesting things to overcome in your relationships.

4. *What does this person need from me?*
   Relationships are two-way streets. You need something from the other character; at the same time, the other character needs something from you. You must stay open and discover what the other character needs from you during the scene.

5. *What is my history with this person?*
   Discover or invent something from the past that might affect or color the current situation.

6. *What do I see as my future with this person?*
   Imagining the future is even more important than knowing the past. What is it that you want to happen with this person in the immediate and/or the distant future?

7. *How can this person hurt me?*

   Are you vulnerable with this person? Each person is very capable of hurting any other person. This vulnerability often plays an important role in the way a relationship plays out.

Is There Any Love in This Relationship?

Love, or the lack of love, on any level or by any definition is an interesting element in a relationship. Plays are often about people in love or in conflict because of love.

What Roles Do We Play for Each Other?

We all play roles for each other. Plays rely heavily on people playing these roles for each other. The different types of roles are as varied and complicated as the people playing them. They are often determined by the desire of one character that the other character fit into an expected mold, such as that of a slave, mother, yes man, lover, knight in shining armor, best friend, hero, lackey, savior, destroyer, soul mate, etc. Sometimes the desire for another to play a role for you can completely define a relationship.

Two Relationships in One

The one overwhelming thing that both the characters and the actors in a scene have in common is the fact that both are human beings. You can use this commonality to its full advantage in a scene:

Both can be hurt.
Both can be scared.
Both can be inspired.
Both can be befriended.

If your character has to do something to another character, why not as an actor also try to do the same thing to the other actor—unless, of course, it is dangerous, immoral, or illegal! For example, if your character is trying to make the other character fall in love, you make the other actor fall in love with you. If your character is trying to threaten the other character, you threaten the other actor. After the rehearsal, you can say "Just kidding"; but during the rehearsal, don't kid, do.

 ### Relationship Joke Exercise

Choose a story or joke that is at least thirty seconds in duration. Now, tell it to several imagined people or groups, such as:

- Your minister, priest, or rabbi
- Your grandmother
- The President of the United States
- The audience of the Super Bowl half-time show
- Someone you have a crush on
- A pseudo-intellectual
- Your favorite comedian
- Your executioners
- A child
- Your childhood hero

Rope Scene Exercise

You will need a soft cotton rope, 10 to 15 feet long.

Memorize a scene well with your partner. Take the rope and wrap or tie each end around yourselves. As you perform, each of you tries to lead the other or bring the other to you when appropriate. This is effective in scenes in which partners are trying to control or overpower each other.

Be careful with this exercise. I have used it for years and no one has ever gotten hurt, but the potential for injury is there.

Pillow Throw Scene Exercise

You and your partner memorize a short scene. While you are rehearsing the scene, have one very soft pillow. At the end of each line, throw, hit, or hand the pillow to the other person. The action with the pillow should reflect your action goal with the line. So, if you are angry with the other person, let that person have it. If you are comforting that person, hand it over gently.

Insult/Compliment Exercise

While rehearsing a scene, go through it once or twice, saying at the end of the line how your character really feels about the other person at that precise moment. For example:

- "Hi. (Loser.)"
- "Hello. (My hero.)"
- "How are you? (Idiot.)"
- "Oh, just great. (I worship you.)"
- "That's great. (Jerk.)"
- "Thanks. (My god.)"

Connecting Exercise Using a Script

In the early part of a rehearsal, even before you learn your lines, two partners should sit in two straight-backed chairs, facing each other with knees almost or actually touching. Look at each line for as long as necessary. When you are ready, make eye contact with your partner and deliver your line. Try to get a reaction. Do this with each line. Keep eye contact when your partner delivers the line. Try to feel what they are trying to do.

This will take much longer than simply reading the lines to each other, but you will begin to find meaning in the lines. You will start finding the action, you will begin reacting, and you will learn your lines much faster.

The next step, if it is appropriate for your scene, is to reach out and touch the other person with each line, always aiming for a reaction.

 ## Relationship Scene Exercise

Find a partner. Work on this simple relationship scene. Do it several times but each time change the situation—place, relationships, and goal.

Relationship Scene

A: Hello

B: Hello

A : Well

B : How have you been

A : Great and you

B : All right I guess

A : That's great

B : What have you been doing

A : Nothing what about you

B : All sorts of things

A : Really

B : Yes

A : Are you sure

B : Yes

A : Oh I see

B : Well see you later

A : Don't you remember

B : I will always remember

A : Me too

B : Goodbye

A : Yes

B : Yes

 ## Imagined Obstacles Exercise

Do the relationship scene, but this time, add the following imagined obstacles:

- There is a wall between you.
- The "rules say" you cannot speak to each other.
- You are running out of time.
- The other person is very ill.
- You are running out of air.
- You shouldn't be talking to this class or sort of person.
- The other person smells awful.

 ## Imagined Conflicts Exercise

Do the relationship scene again, but add an imagined conflict, such as:

- A needs B to help, but A doesn't like B.
- A wants to be the leader, but so does B.
- A wants B to love him or her; B wants to be left in peace.
- A wants a hug, B wants a handshake.
- A wants to be worshipped, B wants to be worshipped.
- A wants to have fun, B wants to read quietly.

5

Character, Emotion, and the Rehearsal Process

CHARACTER WORK

Finding the Character

There is one overwhelming thing that you and your character have in common: You are both human beings. Human beings all have a potential for weakness or strength, fear or courage, hope or despair, and, placed in similar situations, we all often behave and react similarly. As a result, always approach your character through the situation.

The best place to start finding your character is to start with the old Stanislavsky *magic if*: If I were in this situation, how would I feel and what would I do? You must always start from yourself. Put yourself in the character's situation and try to relate.

Now, the rub is: What is situation? Situation is everything—absolutely everything—that has an effect upon the character's needs, physical actions, and emotional state. When you get into your character's situation, you must explore everything about the situation, from the past, present, and future. This next exercise can help you understand your character's universe (also known as *your situation*), or the world that the playwright has created for your character.

Given Situation Sheet

Divide a piece of paper into three sections and label them:

Character	Me	Relate, substitute, or research

Go through the script. In the character column, write down:

- Everything the playwright says about the character.
- Everything the character says about him- or herself.
- Everything the other characters say about the character.

After you fill out the character column, fill in the "Me" column, writing about your own life experiences.

In the third column, write down whether you personally relate to what the character is experiencing, whether you must research the experience, or whether you can substutute this experience for one of your own. You may also write down any impressions you may have about the character's situation that are not obviously stated, but could be implied. Write down anything that has affect on the situation. When going through the script also be aware of anything that various characters (or even your character) say that may not be true.

Take for example the play *Hamlet*.

Character	Me	Relate, substitute, or research
Prince of Denmark	Acting student	Sometimes when I have a lead in a play, I almost feel like royalty. (substitute)
Lives in the early 17th century	I live in the early 21st century	Must research customs, movement, history of late 16th, early 17th century. (research)
Has trouble with stepfather/uncle.	I have a stepfather	I am often jealous of my stepfather. (relate)

Relating

More often than not, you will find you relate, or have things in common, with your character. That is, again, because you and your characters do have one overwhelming thing in common: You are both human beings.

As a human, you view the world with many, if not most, of the same wants, needs, insecurities, and fears as your character. Always start from the point of finding how much you and your character are alike. Of course, the best place to start is with the *magic if*. If you were in this situation, how would you feel and what would you *do*? Be careful and think it all the way through.

When you find you have related with a character thoroughly, take time to consider everything. Look at all the information you are given and consider everything. Here is an example:

Several years ago, I played the role of Dylan Thomas in the play *Dylan*. Dylan Thomas was the great Welsh lyric poet who died from complications related to alcoholism before he was 40. In the opening scene, he is on a beach, and he has just had a big fight with his wife, Caitlin. The fight was a result of the fact that the next day he was leaving for a long reading tour in America. His wife feels completely abandoned; there is very little money and she has no one to help her with their children.

I felt I completely related to this scene. Several times, I had to leave my girlfriend or my wife to take an acting or directing job. Every time I left, there was an argument. I had lived almost this exact scene several times. I thought I related to this completely. However, what I missed were the children. The guilt in leaving one's significant other is one thing. Leaving your kids is a whole different story. At the time, I had no children. I now do. Now, I would play this scene completely differently. Now, I could relate to the whole scene. Then, I was only relating with a part of it; I hadn't thought it completely through. I needed to do some more thinking, research, and/or substitution for the relationship of a father and his children.

Substituting

You substitute by creating or remembering an experience from your life that is similar but not exactly the same as your character's experience. For instance, a beach in Northern California might substitute for a beach in Wales. Your pet might create a strong enough emotion to substitute for your character's children. Apple cider, instead of apple juice, may be strong enough to substitute for the taste of whiskey. In a sense, you are trying to trick yourself to respond in an empathetic manner to what your character is experiencing. My two favorite substitution stories are these:

A young woman was rehearsing a directed scene. The scene revolved around her fawning over a baby in a crib, and she seemed detached, almost bored. The fact was that this woman didn't really like children, especially babies. The next time she worked on the scene, the director placed a very large diamond bracelet on the pillow in the crib. When the young woman saw it, she played the scene with surprise, joy, and great interest.

This story has become almost urban legend among directors. Whether it is true or not it still serves a great point.

My all-time favorite substitution story comes from the respected actor Bruce Dern, father of Laura Dern, and a wonderful acting teacher. He was in a play in which he played a young man in Ireland. In several scenes, he was supposed to carry a homemade bomb. This bomb, of course, could go off at any time. Instead of just pretending he was carrying a bomb, he chose to borrow several very fine and expensive crystal glasses that belonged, I believe, to his mother-in-law. He wrapped them in newspaper and put them in the bag supposedly containing the bomb. He said if those glasses had broken, it would have been worse than a bomb blowing up.

Researching

This, to me, is the fun part of acting. You get to find out about parts of the world you might never otherwise experience.

There are two types of research: *in a chair* or *on your feet*. *In a chair* research is done by reading books, letters, diaries; watching films; viewing art pieces; and talking to people about your character and your character's world.

On your feet research is when you get up and live your character's life. You research by actually doing those things that most influence your character's wants, needs, and behavior. We have all heard stories of actors riding along with police officers when preparing for a police show, of Robert DeNiro getting a taxi license when doing research for *Taxi Driver*, or of Robert Duvall writing country western songs for *Tender Mercies*. This type of research on a character's life is sometimes invaluable. There is no substitution for real experience.

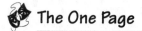 ## The One Page

Who, What, Where, When, and Why Sheet

Sometimes it is helpful to have one page at which you can glance to get a brief, overall understanding of the character situations.

Take a legal size (or larger) piece of paper and label it the Who, What, Where, When, and Why Sheet.

Simply write down anything you find in the script or any impression you have that can influence your character. Keep it as simple and concise as possible because this is only an overview. There is no right or wrong way to do this.

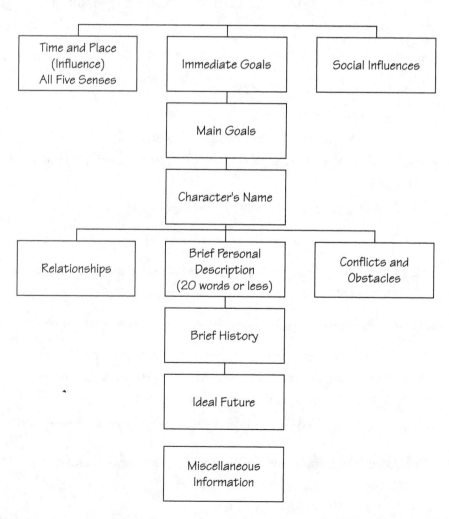

Questions and Considerations

Time and Place

- What is it about the time that influences you?
- What in this place influences you?
- What do you feel, hear, smell, taste, and see? How do these things influence you?

Immediate Goals

- Go through the script and break it into small sections. End each section when you have won or lost a definite want or need.

Social Influences

- Is this a peaceful or chaotic time?
- Does it matter what other people think?
- What is the expected behavior of this time?
- Does class, religion, employment, or social standing influence you?
- What is your relationship with society?

Main Goals

- In order to live happily ever after, what is the one main thing that you must do?

Character's Name

- Know your character's full name. If it is not given to you in the script make it up yourself. How do you feel about your name? How does it influence you?

Relationships

- List each character with whom you have an important relationship.

- What do you need from each of these characters? Do your needs change during the course of the play?

Brief Personal Description

- How do you dress?
- What do you look like?
- What unique aspects of your look and dress influence your behavior and self-esteem?

Conflicts and Obstacles

- What things are in your way? How?
- What people are in your way? How?
- What are you going to do about these problems?

Brief History

- What are the main events and people from your past that make you the way you are today?

Ideal Future

- How do you want things to turn out?
- What do you expect to happen?
- How much do you want or need these things?

Miscellaneous Information

- This is a place to write down anything not covered elsewhere. Note images or thoughts.

Situation and Other Characters

Without a doubt, the one situational factor that will influence and create your character the most is how that character feels and acts around the various other characters. For instance, if your character feels another character is smarter than he or she, he or she may well feel stupid. In contrast, if your character feels the other character is stupid, he or she may feel smarter this time.

To play a superior type person you only have to feel everyone is your inferior and react and treat them that way. In contrast, to play a weak character you need only to imagine that everyone is stronger; in other words, you react or play against whatever the other characters are playing or representing. You believe in the situation as presented to you by the other characters and actors. You then stay alive and real in that belief.

Belief in the other character(s) and focusing your goals on those characters will give your character focus and purpose. It will define who you are and how you behave. It is not as important that you believe you are Juliet as it is that you believe the young man you are talking to in the scene is Romeo. This concept of believing in the other characters and focusing your goals on them is called *playing the other*, or *playing the opposite*. For a broader presentation of this concept, I highly recommend *Acting One* or *Acting Power* by my graduate directing and acting teacher, Robert Cohen.

Character Day Exercise

A week or two before your class presents scenes, you and your classmates should spend the entire class period as your characters. From the moment you enter until you leave (even during the break), you need to stay in character. During this time, your instructor asks questions about your characters, such as:

- What is your full name?
- Tell us about yourself in fifty words or less.
- What is your biggest problem?

Next, open up the discussion so that the characters can ask other characters questions. It gets very interesting when Romeo asks Stanley Kowalski for tips about a woman or St. Joan asks Blanche Dubois if she also hears voices.

Character Letter

Write a letter from your character to you, the actor. The character should tell you those aspects of his or her personality, situation, and problems on which you should concentrate. The character can tell you secrets and share with you things about his or her past and desires for the future.

You can also write back with your plan on how you intend to discover and use your own personality and life experiences to capture the essence of the character.

 ## Relationship Letter

As your character, write a detailed letter to the other characters in the script with which you have the most important interactions. Tell them what you need from them, how you feel about them, what your biggest problems with them are, and what you hope your future is with them. If it is appropriate for your character, actually mail the letter. If not, lock it away and refer to it occasionally.

Character Meal

Go out to lunch or dinner as your character. This can be done alone or with other cast members or your director. Stay in character the entire meal. Of course, this might be problematic if you are playing a sociopath or antisocial character. Use your own judgment and don't get into trouble, but remember, even villains have to eat. Sweeney Todd must have had fish and chips and Hannibal Lecter probably had a cheeseburger sometimes. Bon appetit!

EMOTIONS

First and foremost, if you are really in the situation (in character) the emotions will be the right emotion for the situation.

Second, emotion is never a goal. Emotion is a result. Emotions happen because of expectations. They happen because your character is in the situation and is pursuing goals. Through the pursuit of goals, the character is either frustrated or satisfied. Emotion is a result of a frustrated or satisfied expectation.

Make your emotion important. If you are not feeling any strong emotion in a scene, then chances are you are not connected or in the situation; or you have not really looked at the situation and made the desires and expectations strong enough. If your character wants and expects something enough, emotion will come. If this is not happening, then you need to reexamine the situation and somehow make it more important, more desired, or more expected.

However, sometimes, you may have to go into a scene cold or you may have some sort of an emotional block. Here are a few tricks or techniques on how to get physical and use your imagination that can help you break through your emotional block.

Get Physical

Have you ever watched a football game? It is amazing how a group of normally reserved, often repressed people can suddenly become emotional maniacs; hugging, yelling, jumping up and down, even crying. Why? There are two reasons:

Reason number one: There are obvious and important goals that are being met or frustrated.

Reason number two: Their bodies are into it. Through the running, jumping, hitting, yelling, and cursing, their bodies are emotionally charged and accessible.

Go team, go!
You @!&%$#!*

This same type of physicality can work for an actor. Never jump into a scene physically cold. Run, jump, stretch, yell, or do whatever you can think of to get your body going and involved in what you are doing.

— *Physical action can stimulate emotion.* —

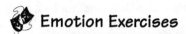 ## Emotion Exercises

Exercise #1: Run

Just before your scene, go for a quick 200-yard run, then begin the scene.

Exercise #2: Mime Show

Do your scene without words. Exaggerate each movement.

Exercise #3: Mime Fight

You and your partner stand ten to fifteen feet apart. As you say each line, physically act out your subtext without touching your partner.

Have a fight from that distance. Kick, hit, and claw the other person (without touching).

Exercise #4: Vent

Before a scene, vent all your character's and your own frustration on an object like a soft couch, a punching bag, a pillow, or a doll. Really let go. Let everything out.

Exercise #5: Tug-of-War

You and your partner have a real or imaginary tug-of-war while saying the lines.

Exercise #6: Play a Game

You and your partner play racquetball, tennis, handball, or any other appropriate game as you are saying the lines. Let the game and lines affect each other.

Exercise #7: Breathe

Breathing may seem simple enough, but it can be the key to real physical and emotional involvement in a scene.

Just before you begin a scene, make yourself breathe the way the character is breathing in the situation. At first, just fake it to get your breath going. After a while, if your breathing is right and you are involving yourself physically in the situation, the sorts of emotions one might expect in such a situation will soon follow.

Exercise #8: Use Your Memories

If you have had an experience in your past that is similar to what your character is going through, why not use it? Draw upon how you felt and reacted during that past experience. If you are capable and brave enough to do this, it can be an invaluable resource. Go back in your memory and try to relive the experience as specifically as you can. Make mental notes of what you can use and put aside the rest. It is best to use memories that have real meaning and that are emotionally loaded but over which you also have control. It is important that you are able to control and use your past emotional memories and then able to let them go back to being memories in the past. For this reason, you should avoid experiences that are either too traumatic or too recent for you to have a good objective perspective.

Use Your Imagination

What makes some people seem so talented as actors is in reality their talent for empathy. Often these people don't have to actually have experienced something;. they simply can almost completely put themselves into a situation. These people have great sensitivity and great imagination. If you possess these qualities, why not use them in your preparation work? Let your imagination and sensitivity go. Daydream, fantasize, be childlike and make-believe. If such fantasizing can produce emotions and other qualities you can use in your acting, by all means use them.

Emotional Imagination Exercises

Exercise #1

Watch people and let your imagination go as you watch them. Imagine their world and their lives. Where did they just come from? Where are they going? What if you went with them? What if something extreme happened to them?

But this is the tenth time you've seen My Dog Skip.

Exercise #2

Clip a picture out of a magazine. Imagine yourself in that world.

Exercise #3

Look at an art book or go to a museum. Find one picture with a great deal of action. Imagine yourself in that picture and feel the emotions growing inside yourself.

REHEARSAL TECHNIQUES THAT WORK

Rehearsing any scene is a process. Take it step by step. Do not try for results right away. Going for results and trying to rush the rehearsal process always produces flat, one-dimensional, boring characters and scenes.

1. *First Step.*

   Read the script by yourself. Try to read the whole script if it is available. If you can read it in one sitting, so much the better. Write down any impressions you have. Often, first impressions are instinctively correct.

2. *Second Step.*

   Meet with your partner. Read the scene. Briefly discuss your ideas about the scene, hitting on all the goals, obstacles, and relationships that you discover in the scene. Discuss any environmental or physical influences on the scene in depth.

3. *Third Step.*

   Work on connection. Sit in a chair directly facing your partner. Break lines up into small segments. While making eye contact, deliver the line to your partner. Try to connect with your partner and get a reaction from him or her with each line. Take your time and even repeat lines when needed.

4. *Fourth Step.*

   Break the scene into small sections (usually each with one immediate goal). Work on these sections first through improvisation then by adding the script dialogue.

5. *Fifth Step.*

   Work on the scene using imagined improvisations. If appropriate, improvise scenes from the characters' relationship. For instance, if the scene on which you are working is about a couple breaking up, improvise a scene about when the couple first met or how the couple interacts an average day.

6. *Sixth Step.*

   With your partner, take a field trip as your characters. Go out to lunch, have a picnic, play a game, or do something else that is appropriate for your characters.

7. *Seventh Step.*

   Start putting the scene together and begin run throughs.

8. *Eighth Step.*

   Tear the scene apart. Now that you have begun to set things up, upset them. Play. Let your imagination take over.

Using the lines and situation:

Play chess.
Go for a jog.
Goof around.
Play tennis.
Play Frisbee.
Have a tug-of-war.
Have a pillow fight.
Pretend you are
animals.

Do the scene in
gibberish.

Smile when you say that, partner.

Pretend you are a 7 year old.
Play the insult/compliment game.

By playing with the scene, you will find new things you can use to help you in your work, and you will hear words for the first time.

9. *Ninth Step.*

Reread the script as if it is the first time you are reading it. Look for new impressions and anything you may have missed in previous readings.

10. *Tenth Step.*

Perform the scene for an audience. Set only essential elements. Keep flexible parts of the scene in a slightly improvisational state. Actively listen and watch your partner as you perform.

6

Now Add the Audience

GET YOURSELF READY

You need to be at your mental and physical peak at the moment the lights go on or the curtain goes up and the scene begins. To be able to do this you must:

Be well rested.

Be well nourished but not full or digesting a recent meal.

Have had plenty of water before the performance and be prepared to drink plenty of water during the performance.

Put the "outside world" away and concentrate on your character's universe.

Be sure the set or stage is ready.

Be sure your costumes, make-up, and props are ready.

Be vocally and physically warmed-up.

THE LAST 2-3 MINUTES

You must prepare yourself physically, emotionally, and mentally to perform. Never jump into a scene cold. If you start out cold, it will take half the scene to really get going. There are a variety of ways to prepare and center yourself and they should all be done in the two to three minutes before you perform.

How now brown cow.

Calm yourself down by stretching or shaking out.

Concentrate on the beginning moment.

Quickly go through your goals.

Visualize the physical environment.

Put attention on your breath.

Get yourself physically ready to attack the scene.

YOUR RELATIONSHIP WITH THE AUDIENCE

The audience should never be just a distant presence with whom you have no interaction. You must establish a relationship with the people in the seats. If you are in a presentational play, in which the actor actually speaks to the audience, this relationship can be used to great advantage. To develop such a relationship, try imagining the audience as a group of friends, your fan club, a group of coconspirators, a group of people who need convincing, your family, a group of people who hate you, a group of psychologists, a group of children, a lynch mob, or whatever other sort of group might

bring out qualities that you wish in your character or that you think will help create interesting situations.

Listen for or imagine reactions from the audience, and respond to them. Even if you are in a representational play, in which the audience does not take an active part, you can draw upon the audience's reactions. They can be that group of people we all carry around in our head, the ones from whom we seek approval or are trying to impress. They can be a judgemental society, your conscience, or whatever else will work for your character's situation.

Never let the audience be neutral. Let them root for you, challenge you, support you, and inspire you.

 ## Imagined Active Audience Exercise

Take anything you have memorized, a monologue, song lyric, poem, fairy tale, anything. Now, imagine you are addressing an audience with your memorized piece. Address different types of audiences, such as:

- A group of polite children
- A group of loud, obnoxious children
- A group of people who don't believe you
- A group of people who are going to vote for you
- A group of intellectuals
- A group of very slow people
- A group of friends
- Your family
- "The Committee"
- All of your ex-boyfriends or girlfriends

 ## Actual Active Audience Exercise

This can be either a partner or group exercise. One person presents a memorized monologue or soliloquy. This works best on speeches spoken directly to the audience, but it can work to some degree on any speech. The partner or group listens to the monologue, but instead of being polite, quiet listeners, the partner or group becomes very active, verbally and physically reacting to what the person on stage is saying. The person delivering the monologue in turn reacts (using the monologue) to whatever is being done or said by the audience. To this, the partner or group should respond with such phrases as:

- You're right!
- You can say that again!
- What are you talking about?
- Hooray!
- Amen, brother!
- Liar!
- Bull!
- That's the truth!
- Bring it home, baby!

The partner or group can respond physically by applauding occasionally, getting up to leave, throwing soft things (like socks, pillows, or nerf balls), or by turning away. To the responses of the audience, the person delivering the monologue can physically react and adjust accordingly from moment to moment.

7

Tips, More Advice, Secrets, Things That Work, Strange Things Actors Do, and a Few Final Words

A LIST OF TIPS

1. *California Line Endings.*

   I have called this type of line ending a California line ending for years, although I have also heard them in West Virginia, New York City, and on most television shows. It is also called a *downward line ending*, and it occurs when the last few words in a line lose volume, intensity, or energy. This loss of intensity usually means the actor is not going for his goal in that line. It can cause a scene to lose energy and if done in repetition it can almost have a hypnotic effect. The last few words of a line are always important. They must have at least as much energy as the rest of the lines and usually a bit more.

2. *The "I" Point.*

   In real life we may use the word "I" several times in a conversation and never once point at ourselves. In a scene, most actors can't resist pointing at themselves each time they utter the word "I." Try saying lines like:

I'm going to the store.

Because I want some ice cream.

I think I will get chocolate.

Because chocolate is my favorite.

Try pointing at yourself on every "I," "I'm," and "my." See how silly it seems when you are aware of pointing to yourself. There are, of course, times you may wish to point to yourself for great emphasis, but those times are rare and are usually done for great effect.

3. *Charm.*

   The one thing that all great actors have in common is their ability to charm the other characters, actors, and audience. It is the combination of active outward energy, the ability to act interested in other people, and humility. Always look for the charm in your characters and always use your own charming qualities.

4. *Smile.*

   Never, ever underestimate the power of smiling. It can be a potent weapon for any type of character. It shows you are in control. You are enjoying the moment. A smile can also draw the audience toward you.

   I was once playing a lead in a musical. I was working very hard and I thought I fully understood the character. I also felt that the audience just didn't like me for some reason. A friend of mine, who is a respected and famous actor, saw my performance. I asked him, "Why can't I reach the audience?" He said one word. "Smile."

   The next night I purposely tried to smile when I could and when I felt it was appropriate. After the performance—and after a standing ovation—the director came up to me and asked, "What happened, you were one hundred percent better tonight. The audience *loved* you." I just said, "I tried smiling."

Try it yourself. You might even join the ranks of great smilers like Katherine Hepburn, Tom Cruise, and Jack Nicholson.

5. *Sighing.*

Usually, one of the worst choices an actor can make is to sigh before or after saying a line. A sigh releases both your and the audience's energy. For that few seconds, you drop out of the scene. You have to inhale again before you re-enter the scene. Oh, of course, there are times when a sigh may be very effective, but use those moments judiciously.

6. *Grapefruit Acting.*

Picture two actors facing each other. They are both trying to make a strong point. One (or sometimes both) will stand with hands out in front of the body—palms out and fingers slightly curled—both hands shaking. If you cannot hear the dialogue between the two actors, it looks like the actors are miming "Look at my grapefruits, I am going to shake the juice out of them," or "I just polished my nails and they won't dry."

In real life I've never seen people hold their hands in this way, but in acting class it happens daily. It happens because the actor is not really connecting with the other actor and has excess energy

that he or she is unable to direct. Gestures must be directed outward toward another person or must be used to help explain a point to another person.

7. *Bruise Acting.*

At the end of a line (and occasionally during one) some actors let their hand fall almost violently toward their thighs or hips. I have known some actors to do it so with much energy and so often that they give themselves bruises. This is an undirected release of physical energy. It always indicates to me that you are not directing your concentration and goals to your scene partner and that your attention is remaining on yourself.

8. *In to Out.*

Emotions and action originate internally but ultimately move outward toward the other people in the scene. It is important that you feel an emotion, but it is much more important that you deliver that emotion and try to do something with it that affects the others in the scene.

9. *Commit.*

When you are in a scene you must commit to the situation one hundred percent. Go for it! Believe in what you are doing.

10. *Do Not Comment on a Character.*

This goes along with committing to a scene. When you take on a character, even if that character is one that makes you uncomfortable or even disgusts you, you must be that character without judgment or without showing your discomfort to the audience.

11. *Find All Sides of the Character.*

Never play a hero as if he is only a hero. Never play a villain as if he is only a villain. Find the good, the bad, and the ugly in each and every character.

12. *Play the Comedy with the Serious and Vice Versa.*

    If you are playing in a tense drama, find the humor in the scene. If you are in a comedy, find what is serious about a situation. This will almost automatically add an interesting dimension to your scene.

13. *Don't Indicate.*

    Indicating is what you do when you show the audience what you are feeling or thinking. Don't ever show, just do and trust that your feelings and thoughts will be discovered by the audience.

14. *Projection and Articulation as a Tool.*

    Never be loud just so the audience can hear you. Be loud and clear so your universe and the other characters (which includes the audience) understand every word you are saying. Make everything you are saying important enough that you want it to be understood by the other characters clearly.

15. *Rehearsal Attitude.*

    Go into each rehearsal with the same energy and commitment as a performance. Rehearsals are not only times to work on character and situations, they are also times to present all that you have been working on outside of rehearsal.

16. *Play the Human Being.*

    I have discussed this in the relationship section; however, it is important so I want to bring it up again. The main thing the actor and the character have in common is that both are human beings. You can manipulate, stimulate, and relate to other human beings. Play the human being, not his or her character.

17. *The Magic If.*

    Always start with:

    > If I were in this situation what would I do?

> If he or she really were (the other character's name),
> how would I relate with that person?

You must bring your experience, emotions, and understanding to the character you are playing. Remember that both you and the character are feeling, living, hoping human beings. This is where you must always start.

18. *Never Give Up.*

The main fuel of the character is struggle. Characters must continue to strive to reach their goals until the last word of the last line. Always assume, or at least have hope, that you will eventually win as a character.

19. *Crescendos.*

In music, a crescendo is a slow, steady rise in volume and intensity. Using a crescendo on a line can be very effective. It shows that you really mean what you are saying. It is especially effective in any type of list or building phrase. For example,

> I want you to go. I want you to go now. I want you to go
> right now!

It is implied here that each sentence is more intense than the next. Many actors will miss this very dramatic and effective opportunity.

Using a crescendo may seem like a very technical approach to a line. It is. However, it is also a tactic that is used all the time in real life among people who really know what they want. Playwrights are aware of this. You will find these crescendo lists in almost every play ever written.

20. *Don't Censor Yourself.*

Plays are often about people wanting very basic things. As a result, they are often about love, sex, power, greed, and fear. To communicate such strong and sometimes base emotions and values, you as an actor must be willing to think the unthinkable. You must be able to go into places in your mind that most people do not wish to visit.

When reaching for these places in your mind, don't get in your own way. Remember that these dark places only exist in your thoughts or fantasies. For these situations, it's okay to give in to the dark side. After rehearsal, just let these thoughts and fantasies go. If you can create a thought, you can also let go of it. It is the responsibility of an actor to be able to make-believe and then to let it go.

21. Energy.

Acting is all about passionate, physical energy. Energy comes from desire. It comes from a combination of the actor's desire to communicate with the audience and the character's and actor's desire to accomplish strong goals.

22. Faster, Funnier, Louder!

The great Broadway producer and director George Abbot used to say that he always had to make every play on which he ever worked faster, funnier, and louder. For you as an actor to do this means in a sense that you must give your character more energy. In fact, every actor in the production must give his or her character more energy for the show to be faster, funnier, and louder. Energy comes from a character's desire, as mentioned in tip number 21; and to satisfy that desire you must use everything you have, including wit, humor, and charm to get what you want. One of the ways you make sure everyone understands what you really want is to become faster, funnier, and louder!

23. Know When to Be Plain and When to Be Vain.

Many actors only want to look their best when on stage or in front of a camera. Such a value on one's appearance is terrific when it is called for, but if it is not appropriate, you must be willing to look like your character should look in the situation.

You are portraying a living, real person, not trying out for a beauty contest.

That may be a bit too much makeup for the Oregon Trail.

24. *Actively Doing Nothing.*

Acting is not always performing. Sometimes it means just being on stage or in front of the camera. However, that doesn't mean you are doing nothing. You are always doing something because you are always actively listening and watching. Don't feel you always have to be "on" by mugging or flailing your arms about. Don't feel the focus always has to be on you. Just live in the situation and respond to what you must to get what you want. Less is often more.

25. *Make Sure You Have an Audience.*

If you do a strong physical action that is for the benefit of the other character(s) in the scene, make sure they see you do it. Never do an action that is not somehow connected to the characters in the scene or the seated audience.

What is juror #4 doing?

26. *Don't Get in the Way of the Story.*

   As an actor, you are a storyteller first and last. Everything
   you do is for the purpose of telling the story. Every choice you
   make must be made with that in mind. Stay away from anything that will detract from furthering the plot and the audience's understanding of your character.

A FEW FINAL WORDS ABOUT LEARNING TO ACT

Making Mistakes

In performance, you want to keep your mistakes to a minimum. In
rehearsal and acting classes, go ahead and make mistakes. Make
big mistakes! Mistakes come from experimenting and trying things
beyond your capabilities. This is the only way we grow.

Looking Foolish

This is the actor's job, isn't it? You must be ready to look foolish to
a certain percentage of the audience or the actors at anytime. If
you are willing to play the fool once and a while you will find true
creative freedom and the joy of performing.

Be Bored, Enjoy the Silence, and Think about Yourself Once and a While

It is all well and good to work and study with great passion and energy. But you must from time to time stop, regroup, think about
your life and art, and sometimes just get downright bored. It is in
these moments we grow as artists and human beings. Analyze and
reevaluate what you have been doing and prioritize what you need
and want to do.

Be More Interested in Process and Less in Results

We live in a society obsessed with instant gratification. We want everything now! Instant gratification is fine for most people. Let those people have their microwave ovens and express lanes. Artists and other creative people need to slow down. Enjoy the task or trip, not just the completion or arrival. Acting is always about process.

Stretching Yourself

Choose roles and actions that will make you grow. When in an acting class, tackle the type of material with which you are not comfortable or that is downright difficult for you. Never settle for what you might consider just good enough. Always go a little farther than you think you can. Always challenge yourself. Challenges will keep you fresh, constantly interested in your craft, and will help you reach your potential.

— Break a leg! —

Index